# CHRISTIAN LIFE

## BY KEN CHANT

# CHRISTIAN LIFE

# By Dr. Ken Chant

Copyright © 2012 Ken Chant

ISBN 978-1-61529-036-9

Vision Publishing
1672 Main St. E 109
Ramona, CA 92065
1-800-9-VISION
**www.booksbyvision.com**

## A NOTE ON GENDER

It is unfortunate that the English language does not contain an adequate generic pronoun (especially in the singular number) that includes without bias both male and female. So *"he, him, his, man, mankind,"* with their plurals, must do the work for both sexes. Accordingly, wherever it is appropriate to do so in the following pages, please include the feminine gender in the masculine, and vice versa.

## FOOTNOTES

A work once fully referenced will thereafter be noted either by "ibid" or "op. cit."

# CONTENTS

# ABBREVIATIONS

Abbreviations commonly used for the books of the Bible are

| | | | |
|---|---|---|---|
| Genesis | Ge | Habakkuk | Hb |
| Exodus | Ex | Zephaniah | Zp |
| Leviticus | Le | Haggai | Hg |
| Numbers | Nu | Zechariah | Zc |
| Deuteronomy | De | Malachi | Mal |
| Joshua | Js | | |
| Judges | Jg | | |
| Ruth | Ru | Matthew | Mt |
| 1 Samuel | 1 Sa | Mark | Mk |
| 2 Samuel | 2 Sa | Luke | Lu |
| 1 Kings | 1 Kg | John | Jn |
| 2 Kings | 2 Kg | Acts | Ac |
| 1 Chronicles | 1 Ch | Romans | Ro |
| 2 Chronicles | 2 Ch | 1 Corinthians | 1 Co |
| Ezra | Ezr | 2 Corinthians | 2 Co |
| Nehemiah | Ne | Galatians | Ga |
| Esther | Es | Ephesians | Ep |
| Job | Jb | Philippians | Ph |
| Psalm | Ps | Colossians | Cl |
| Proverbs | Pr | 1 Thessalonians | 1 Th |
| Ecclesiastes | Ec | 2 Thessalonians | 2 Th |
| Song of Songs | Ca * | 1 Timothy | 1 Ti |
| Isaiah | Is | 2 Timothy | 2 Ti |
| Jeremiah | Je | Titus | Tit |
| Lamentations | La | Philemon | Phm |
| Ezekiel | Ez | Hebrews | He |
| Daniel | Da | James | Ja |
| Hosea | Ho | 1 Peter | 1 Pe |
| Joel | Jl | 2 Peter | 2 Pe |
| Amos | Am | 1 John | 1 Jn |
| Obadiah | Ob | 2 John | 2 Jn |
| Jonah | Jo | 3 John | 3 Jn |
| Micah | Mi | Jude | Ju |
| Nahum | Na | Revelation | Re |

*Ca* is an abbreviation of *Canticles*, a derivative of the Latin name of the *Song of Solomon*, which is sometimes also called the *Song of Songs*.

# PREFACE

# THE HAPPY CHRISTIAN!

Here is an arresting description of a well-balanced Christian:

> *"Happy is the man who has no reason to condemn himself for what he allows" (Ro 14:22).*

If the goal of all life is to achieve happiness, then Paul has revealed one of the key factors in that achievement: happiness is reaching that place of inner poise where you know exactly what is permissible for you, so that you live free from the misery of self-condemnation.

> Now that is a most desirable state, although it is one that few Christians reach. Are you happy in the things you allow or disallow yourself? Or are you continually swinging from acceptance to accusation, from pleasure to disgust, from liking your life-style to despising it?

Do you live comfortably and pleasantly with yourself, your neighbour, and your God; or are you haunted by an uneasy sense of disharmony, of being unsure of yourself, not knowing what you should approve or disapprove, nor how you should relate to the world and the things that are in it? Can you eat, drink, love, laugh, cry, work, play, with contentment and peace, or is your conscience often unsettled, plagued with guilt, restless and troublesome?

Do you love yourself or loathe yourself?

The purpose of this book is to analyse the components of a true Christian life-style, to discover what factors enable the Christian to determine what is allowable, so that you may live without guilt, enjoying fully the happiness which is your God-given right.

# ALTERNATIVE LIFE-STYLES

The major obstacle many Christians face when they attempt to structure their lives is how to choose between the many alternatives that are offered to them.

Those alternatives arise from two sources -

## The Pressures Of Group Conformity

Some churches and denominations demand from their members conformity to certain written or assumed rules which establish among their people an easily recognisable identity. These mores, laws, and traditions, control the life-style of every member in the group. Where this required identity suits the nature of the person affected, where it is flexible enough to allow freedom of conscience and behaviour, or where it does not inhibit the expression of God's purpose through any person, there is no harm in it; on the contrary it helps to establish the homogeneity and cohesiveness of the group.

However, this group pressure often tends to eliminate any real development of character. It can become a dehumanising pressure to conform, an imprisonment of spirit, a reduction of every member in the group to a common denominator. People who are pressed into the fixed mould of the group may find their Christian lives becoming stilted and artificial and they may find themselves locked into a suffocating atmosphere of spiritual restraint.

When customs and forms which do not in themselves have any real spiritual value become compulsory they also become a straitjacket, sapping vitality and preventing people from freely expressing all that is God's unique and personal gift to each one of them.

In groups which have developed this pressure to conform there is no room for the non-conformist. I wonder what they would do with Jesus if he suddenly appeared among them? Probably the same thing the rigid and orthodox conformists did to him in Bible days: either expel him (Lu 9:49-50), or crucify him. Rule-makers never like rule-breakers.

## The True Pattern

Scripture says that Christ is the example we should follow (1 Pe 2:21). In practice this means that you should not come under any control save that of Jesus as he is revealed to you by the Holy Spirit.

But there is a form in which Christ will show himself to you which will be different from his revelation of himself to me or to any other person in the world.

Of course, we all share many common things in our understanding of Christ; but because we are each one of us uniquely different, there is some part of the total beauty of Jesus that is visible **only to your eyes or mine**. The four gospels demonstrate this. How diverse is each writer's view of the Lord! Each places emphasis on a different aspect of his character. Each responds in a different way to the impact and influence of his personality. Each forms a special vision of Christ.

They were free to be different, of course, because up to that time no ecclesiastical hierarchy had determined to a nicety how a proper Christian should think, talk, feel and act! Those strangulating taboos and strictures had not yet been formulated!

But now your deepest quest in life should be to discover **Christ himself**, in the way he chooses to reveal himself to you personally, and then to follow that example alone.

It must be conceded, of course, that young Christians, like infants, may need to cling to older and wiser saints and to submit to authority until they have developed a mature discretion of their own (1 Pe 2:1-3; and cp. He 5:11-14). But the apron strings should be cut as soon as possible.

It seems to me that the role of a good pastor is to nurture the children of God to the point where they can stand by themselves, able to make their own free and responsible decisions about the purpose of God in their lives.

A pastor who keeps his people utterly dependent on him, or who reckons them safe only while they keep his rules, can hardly be said to have produced grown up saints.

## Be True To Yourself

I have observed another problem. Many great Christians have done much harm by their intimate self-disclosures. Every detail of their personal spiritual pilgrimage has been exposed. They withhold nothing, and the underlying assumption on every page is: "This is the way I found God, and this is the way you will find him." The Bible writers were more restrained. They revealed only such things as all Christians in every generation can relate to.

There are times when silence is golden! "He who restrains his lips is prudent ... A prudent man conceals his knowledge ... He who restrains his words has knowledge, and he who has a cool spirit is a man of understanding" (Pr 10:19; 12:23; 17:27,28).

It is a simple fact that I do not relate to God in the same way that you do, nor will the Lord seek an identical response from both of us, nor will he deal with each of us in exactly the same way.

I may learn some things from God's dealings with others, but not everything. Some of God's dealings with me are exclusive. They belong to me alone. They have no value for you. His ways with me and his ways with you are not the same. But Peter's misguided question is still being asked: **"Lord, what about this man?"** And Christ is still replying, **"What is that to you? Follow me!"** (Jn 21:20-22).

The second source of alternative life-styles is found in -

## The Blandishments Of Devotional Writers

You are standing in front of a group of new Christians. They were converted under your ministry a few weeks ago, but now you must leave them. This may well be your last opportunity to address them. What will you say? How can you ensure that they will continue to serve God with joy? What essential truth, what last word of advice, will you leave with them?

You decide to look for guidance in the various devotional books that are currently popular. At once you are confused, for you discover that writers of devotional books are addicted to presenting various life-styles which are each claimed to be the final answer to the problem of how to be a true Christian.

These authors exhort their readers to espouse the "deeper" life, or the "higher" life; or perhaps to embrace the "crucified" life, the "death-to-self" life, the "broken" life, or the "surrendered" life; or it may be to understand "positional truth", or to seize the life of "praise", or to follow this "message" or that!

All of these books exhibit a "final answer" syndrome. They seek to structure each Christian's life around one central idea. They assume that every dilemma can be resolved through the application of a single principle.

## Searching The Books

Nonetheless, since you must leave some good instruction with your flock, you pick up one of them. Ah! This book teaches that God has created us for his glory alone, hence you dare not do anything for your own pleasure. **You finish the book feeling that God has been painted as an egocentric monster.** Perhaps the author forgot that Jesus said, "I came that you might have abundant life."

You try again. You can hardly believe your eyes. The plan this author presents could appeal only to a person who secretly wishes he was born a statue and not a man. It runs something like this: your own life is utterly worthless, so you must be rid of it altogether. Woe to you if you take even a breath in your own strength. Absolutely nothing good is left in you. You must now consciously live every hour in divine strength alone. You dare do nothing, nor want anything, large or small, significant or insignificant, unless you first pray and get a heavenly clearance. Every action every moment must be placed under divine scrutiny and control. You feel this might be a great method for a puppet, but you want your converts to "quit themselves like men."

Once more you reach up to the shelf. This writer declares that the secret of a life of victory is to see that you are already "complete in Christ", free, victorious, whole. Everything you **want** to be you already **are!** This looks more promising. At least the writer is not laying on his readers the unbearable yoke of being miserable when they are happy or dead when they are alive! But hold! Something seems to be missing? A dimension that fills the pages of the NT is lacking here. This book contains no warning against failure, no practical instruction, no recognition of the fact that to be complete in Christ is not the same as being complete in yourself, and to be complete in the heavenlies is not equivalent to being complete on earth. You know that your flock has a righteous standing in heaven, but you are concerned about their practical state on earth. So you must try again.

You take up another book. This one is different. It is the latest book on the market. It has sold half a million copies. Everyone is excited about it. Thirstily you pore over its pages. An hour later there is a stricken look in your eye. You exclaim, "My God! Surely you won't want me to live like **this**!" The book says: every Christian is a walking egomaniac; you must kill this hideous selfishness; so banish the word "I" from your vocabulary; do nothing to please yourself, demand nothing for yourself, give place to everybody, and so eradicate your "ego". This is difficult to do. Very few are successful. "But," says the author, "I have achieved it." What an egocentric **that** man is!

You look through several more books. They all proclaim, "Here is the way, walk ye in it." They all differ. For the average office worker, or housewife, for the ordinary Christian, these brilliant schemes are quite impractical. They may have been successful for their authors. They may suit people whose temperaments are the same as the authors. They may even present ideas that are soundly scriptural. But as universal panaceas they fail, for it is erroneous to suppose that every difficulty faced by the Christian can be resolved by the application of a single rule.

The fact is, no one concept can solve all the problems of all Christians, nor even all the problems of one Christian. Christian life is not so simple. The issues are complex, the needs are various, each person is different, each situation is unique, each temperament is special, and the solutions are diverse.

## Paul's Advice

So you are still searching for a concise parting message to give your young converts. Where can you go? One reference remains: **the Bible**. Pity you hadn't looked there first. For you find there a man who faced your exact problem. It was Paul, who had to instruct a group of converts he might never see again.

In a few words Paul had to convey to his friends the essence of the gospel he had preached to them. What did he say? We are told that he *"strengthened the souls of the disciples, exhorting them to continue in the faith, and saying that through many tribulations we must enter the kingdom of God"* (Ac 14:22; cp. also 20:17-35).

No simplistic answer there! Only steady perseverance in faith, resolute adherence to the truth, and brave endurance of every difficulty!

Paul was no "hobby-horse" preacher. He did not ride one idea to death. He approached Christian life from an extraordinary number of different perspectives. He refused to be tied to one concept as though it alone was the magic wand which would remove every difficulty.

Paul, like the other NT writers, but unlike many modern writers, understood that hobby horses may be fun to ride, but in the end they can't take you anywhere except up and down!

My task in these lessons will not be to present you with my "**final solution**" to your dilemma, but rather to set before you principles that will enable you to discover your own answer. In the process we should gain together an overview of Christian life, of the difficulties that arise, and of at least some of the ways these difficulties can be overcome.

We shall also be looking at various life-styles; that is, the remarkably different ways that Christians, as worshiping and witnessing servants of God, have chosen across the centuries to structure their lives.

# THE CENTRAL PROBLEM

It could be said that the central problem most people face is the problem of **relationships**. This is true even of a person in solitary confinement or marooned on a deserted island. How you look at yourself and at the world around you, how you relate to time and eternity, to heaven and earth, to things material and spiritual - these relationships all determine the measure of happiness you will experience.

For that reason I have chosen to use the idea of relationships as the framework around which to build this study of Christian life. Another framework could have been chosen, and it would have been equally useful. But "relationships" will enable us to explore together all the territory appropriate for our goal of discovering what it means to be "happy" in Christ.

So this course is in three sections, each analysing a different theme

- ♦  living with yourself
- ♦  living with your neighbour
- ♦  living with your God

The following pages are an important introduction to each of those sections -

## Living With Yourself

Here is an inescapable fact: to be ill at ease with yourself is to be out of phase with all of life.

No man can live comfortably with his neighbour if he cannot first live comfortably with himself. Inner harmony is a necessary prelude to social harmony. The sadness of many lives is the disorder and misery that lack of self-acceptance creates. People do not like themselves, and this dislike casts a shadow on all of their relationships.

The man who loathes himself can hardly love his **neighbour**. Hence Norman Geisler once wrote -

> "In brief, a Christian should love himself for three reasons: firstly because he is made in God's image, which is worthy of love whether it is someone else or one's self; second, because self-love is the basis for loving others; third, because God loves us, and if we do not love ourselves then we do not love what God loves."

And another author, unknown to me, wrote -

> "Many true Christians struggle with a 'conviction of sin' that is not from the Holy Spirit but from (Satan) ... If the Spirit of God shows us our shortcomings he will do so in an atmosphere of forgiveness, and purification. He shows us what we are, not to drive us to despair, but to help ... (Satan tries) to get the faithful to analyse themselves in endless repetition, until the scrutiny robs them of self- confidence, leaving no hope for the future. The Spirit of God does not need our introspection to show us what we are. If we want to know our true condition we should look outward and put ourselves in the light

of God. Only in the light of God can we see the true state of our lives."[1]

Certain kinds of public confession of sin should also be recognised as a false practice, and as one which may destroy spiritual vitality. There is hardly a better way than enforced, misdirected public confession of sin to rob a believer of his legitimate sense of self-confidence.

The Holy Spirit, however, is gentle. He fully respects the usual standards of public behaviour, and has regard for our privacy. Unnecessary public display of intimate sins arises from a false piety which is not content with private acknowledgement of guilt, but requires the special humiliation of public confession.

> "When discussing confession of sin to others the Bible exclusively mentions the elders of the church (Ja 5:14-16), men of such spiritual stature that a confession will not shake them nor make them lose their inner peace."

Christ came, according to the gospel, to help you to get yourself together again, to make you personally whole, to bring you into a harmonious relationship with God, yourself, and with the entire creation (excluding, of course, the kingdom of darkness; that is, Satan and his minions.) Paul expressed this idea of total personal wholeness:

> *"May the God of peace sanctify you wholly; and may your entire spirit and soul and body be kept sound and blameless at the coming of our Lord Jesus Christ. He who calls you is faithful, and he will do it" (1 Th 5:23-24).*

---

[1] I have lost the source of this quote. The same author is also the source of the ideas in the following paragraph.

My desire in this section will be to identify several right and wrong methods of fulfilling that prayer in your own life.

## Living With Your Neighbour

The key word in any discussion of our relationships with our neighbours is "submission" - that is, the world's problems arise mainly from people who press to **rule** rather than **serve**.

This study will define the biblical principle of submission, showing you how to apply it to your family, church, and society.

Some teachers have adopted quite extreme positions on the idea of submission, and many Christians are deeply confused about the matter. For this reason I will emphasise in some detail not only the **need for submission, but also, and just as strongly, its proper extent and limitations.**

The Bible always places a boundary on the exercise of human authority. Those who command should not exceed their God-given right. **Those who obey should do so only as far as scripture requires.**

## Living With Your God

The theme here is the structure of your devotional life and of your relationship with God. The question is asked: does God require you to deny life or to affirm it? The answer to this question will highlight two opposing concepts of Christian life: a **life-denying** concept, and a **life-affirming** concept.

This section will also discuss four major devotional patterns that have been followed by the church over the centuries. Almost all Christians may be placed in one of these four categories. We should be content to flourish in the manner that is most congenial to our own temperament and to respect those who adopt a different style.

I have said that the central theme in each of these studies is "relationships". Another way of expressing the same idea would be to say that our theme is "love"; that is

- ♦ learning to love yourself properly
- ♦ learning to love your neighbour properly
- ♦ learning to love God properly

In any case, the aim behind these studies is to produce Christians who are balanced, stable, and assured; people who have learned how to live in easy harmony with themselves, their society, and their God.

If you have not already achieved such a life-style, I pray that the Holy Spirit will enable you to do so through the following pages.

# SECTION ONE

# LIVING WITH YOURSELF

# CHAPTER ONE

# LOVING GOD'S WORLD

The most distressing problems many people face stem from their own inner attitudes, how they relate to themselves.

Sometimes their folly comprises a distorted self-love; or else they indulge in an excess of self-hate.

Still others suffer from a love-hate relationship in which they cannot decide whether they like or loathe themselves.

There are comparatively few who achieve that place of easy and gracious harmony, of balanced well-being, which Paul described by the Greek noun *"epieikeia"*: "Let all men know your *epieikes*" (Ph 4:5).[2]

Translators have difficulty with *epieikeia*, because there is no exact English equivalent. It occurs seven times in the NT, and it is variously translated as: **gentleness, moderation, forbearance, lenience, considerateness, unselfishness, magnanimity, tolerance, fairmindedness, graciousness, big-heartedness.**

In addition, *epieikeia* also has the sense of suitability, patience, probity, clemency, equitableness. Quite a variety!

Perhaps Matthew Arnold came close to capturing the idea Paul was expressing -

---

[2]     Its grammatical form in this place is that of a substantive adjective, which is read as a noun.

"But there remains the question: what righteousness really is? The method, and secret, and sweet reasonableness of Jesus."

That last phrase, "sweet reasonableness," is one that comes very close to the meaning of *epieikeia*. It is the pathway of tolerant moderation. It avoids extremes - or at least, seeks to avoid them, whenever it is sweetly reasonable to do so!

The man who possesses *epieikeia* is magnanimous to himself and others; he is not a fault-finder but a virtue-seeker; there is a graciousness about his life; he walks serenely, a little amused by human follies; he is disposed to be gentle with weakness, lenient with failure, forbearing toward delay, fair-minded toward opposition; he is not harsh nor intolerant, but considerate; he is not governed by emotion alone, nor by cold logic alone; his method, his secret, as it was Christ's is to be ruled by **sweet reason**!

Contrasted with this intelligent moderation, this sweetness and reasonableness, is the life-style of many Christians who settle on one extreme or another, or who fluctuate incessantly between the two. Their lives are unbalanced, immoderate, and lacking grace. They are unhappy with themselves, with God, and with God's world.

I want to look at these extremes in three areas of the Christian's inner personal relationships, and then show you how to negotiate your way through these extremes by choosing the pathway of *epieikeia*.

# YOUR ATTITUDE TO THE WORLD

## The Two Extremes

What a problem "the world" is to many Christians! And what astonishing steps many of them take in an effort to cope with this problem! Those steps veer from <u>an extremity of abuse to an extremity of asceticism.</u>

## There are those who "abuse" the world

The pleasures of eating and drinking, of sex and play, of culture and entertainment, of work and wealth, exercise a compulsive attraction over them. They greedily indulge themselves, denying nothing to their appetites.

The end result of such satiety is self-disgust and the weariness excess brings.

Just as Amnon fell sick because of his passion for Tamar, and violated her, but then found that he despised her - so these abusers of the world lust after their pleasures but then are driven to hate the thing they craved.

Paul describes them:

> *"Brethren, join in imitating me, and mark those who so live as you have an example in us. For many, of whom I have often told you and now tell you even with tears, live as enemies of the cross of Christ. Their end is destruction, their god is their belly, and they glory in their shame, with minds set on earthly things" (Ph 3:17-19).*

The simple fact is, no Christian should be in bondage to any appetite save a hunger for righteousness.

We are called to live as free people in Christ, slaves to nothing but the will of God. The world is there for us to use but not **abuse** - see 1 Co 7:31, AV, "And they that use this world, as not abusing it."

The same passage in the RSV reads: "Those who deal with the world should live as though they have no dealings with it. For the form of this world is passing away."

Christ also said, "Man shall not live by bread alone, but by every word that proceeds from the mouth of God" (Mt 4:4).

## There are those who "abandon" the world

At the opposite extreme from those who too readily give themselves over to worldly pleasures are those who too readily deny themselves pleasures that are lawful - the **ascetics**.

These people try to isolate themselves as much as they can from all that they choose to call 'worldly". They develop a deep sense of guilt over the pleasures of eating and drinking; they spurn cultural and sometimes intellectual development; they are reluctant to devote any time to simple enjoyment of life; they may condemn most forms of entertainment, such as sport, the theatre, music, art, films, fictional literature; wherever they can, they avoid involvement in secular life and ignore any opportunity to hold public office.

They think that this withdrawal from life and from dynamic contact with the society in which they live, is an expression of their full surrender to God; they think that this kind of separation marks them off as exponents of holiness; they believe that it is in harmony with the NT doctrine of sanctification.

But is it?  What does the NT mean when it bids us to be "separate" from the world, to be "users" but not "abusers" of it?

## What "Separation" Means

See 2 Co 6:14-7:1

That passage contains some exciting promises, breathtaking in their sweep, and in the joy they offer.  God says

- ♦ I will live in them and move among them

- ♦ I will be their God

- ♦ they shall be my people

- ♦ I will welcome you

- ♦ I will be a Father to you

- ♦ you shall be my sons and daughters says the Lord God Almighty.

If you think about those promises you will realise how broad is their scope.  To live in fellowship with God, to know the moving of his Holy Spirit, to be recognised as his beloved children, to be welcomed by him, is to have access to every spiritual resource and to be guaranteed an answer to every prayer.

Here is divine provision! Here is all strength and power! Here is care and protection! Here is the anointing of God! Here is fullness of joy! Here is the essence of all that your heart desires!

But the promise is qualified.  Its realisation does not depend solely on God.  The recipients of the promise have a part to play.  The promise belongs specifically to those who heed the injunction:

*"Therefore come out from them, says the Lord, and touch nothing unclean; then I will welcome you ... (vs 17)*

That demand for separation certainly indicts self-indulgent[3] abusers of the world; but when it is rightly understood it just as certainly indicts self-indulgent ascetics.

The true definition of "separation" is given by Paul himself through the rhetorical questions he placed before the Corinthians (vs 14-16) from those questions we learn that we should be -

## 1. <u>Separate From Sin</u>

"What partnership does righteousness have with iniquity?"

It is self-evident that true Christians can never be comfortable with sin. All who name the name of Christ must depart from iniquity. To pursue sin wilfully while claiming salvation in Christ is to risk total alienation from God (He 10:26-31; 12:25). The injunction is urgent: **"pursue holiness, without which no one can see God"**

All that is identified as sin we must abhor and utterly cast off from ourselves. But here arises a difficulty. Sin, we are told, is very **deceitful**. It is easy to become hardened by this deceitfulness so that sin is no longer recognised as such.

---

[3]  I was about to write "self denying ascetics", but a second thought caused me to change the adjective to self-indulgent", for both groups do in fact yield a larger obedience to the demands of the carnal nature than they do to the demands of scripture. Neither the abuser nor the ascetic is true to God's will. Perhaps it should be mentioned also that I am using the word "ascetic" in a general way to describe any Christian who withdraws from the world to an excessive extent; that is, a Christian who has a false idea of what it means to be "worldly" and "holy". Some forms of asceticism are plainly from God. John the Baptist, for example, was an ascetic; but he, and others like him, fall into a special category, and their asceticism arises from a specific command of God, a divine call.

I have known people to become so deluded by their own self-justifications that, to them, lying is preferable to truth, adultery becomes pure, cheating is exonerated, slander becomes honourable, and God himself is made the author of their iniquities. They turn righteousness into sin and sin into righteousness.

Perhaps you think that is an exaggeration? But the apostle gives a strong warning against this very peril:

> *"Exhort one another every day, as long as it is called 'today', that none of you may be hardened by the deceitfulness of sin. For we share in Christ, if only we hold our first confidence firm to the end"* (He 3:13-14).

If you want to avoid becoming unknowingly enmeshed in sin, the rule is simple: **cleave to the scriptures**. Do not be governed by your own feelings or rationalisations, nor by any voice or impulse which speaks contrary to scripture. The Bible, wisely and responsibly interpreted, is the only reliable guide to righteousness:

> *"All scripture is inspired by God and profitable for teaching, for reproof, for correction, and for training in righteousness, that the man of God may be complete, equipped for every good work"* (2 Ti 3:16-17).

Resolve, **at the deepest level of your being**, that you will be governed by scripture alone; that the single authority over your life will be God's word; and that you will heed only those voices which speak in harmony with the Bible.

Admittedly, that resolution is easier to make than keep, for there are many instructors (among them this Chapter!) which seek to interpret scripture to the people of God - some truly, and some falsely. Each one of us is also capable of reading the Bible through the distorted perspective of prejudice and self-will, thus extracting from the sacred page ideas that are foreign to it.

Evasion of deception by false teachers, by self-delusion, or by immature understanding, depends finally upon the growth of wisdom that experience brings. But a firm commitment to make scripture alone your real mentor is the best beginning toward attaining that wisdom.

## 2. <u>Separate From Darkness</u>

"What fellowship does light have with darkness?"

### A) <u>Do not love the world</u>

"Darkness" may be a synonym for many things, but I am going to limit it here to that aspect of "the world" which John referred to when he wrote -

> *"Do not love the world or the things in the world. If any one loves the world, love for the Father is not in him. For all that is in the world, the lust of the flesh, and the lust of the eyes, and the pride of life, is not of the Father but is of the world. And the world passes away, and the lust of it; but he who does the will of God abides for ever" (1 Jn 2:15-17).*

We are told not to love the world. But what world? The world of politics, art, music, sport, literature, science, school, family, government?

Before we can be separated, we must know precisely what we are to separate from. Nor are we left to guess. John himself defines the "world" he is talking about: it is the "world" that contains **"the lust of the flesh, the lust of the eye, and the pride of life."**

"Lust" and "pride" - those are the characteristics of the world toward which the Christian's heart must remain cold. It is the world of fornication, of malice, of covetousness, of arrogant self-will. It is the world produced by Satanic wiles and human rebellion. It is the world antagonistic to the goodness of God, scorning the mandate he has given the human race to go and subdue the earth and to fill it with fruitfulness.

All that men do in obedience to that mandate, or in the proper use of God's gifts, whether done consciously or unconsciously, is excluded from this God-rejected world. In other words, the expression "world" is used here in a limited sense. It does not mean the whole earth and all that is in it, but only that part of human society and behaviour that is at war with God.

Paul offers similar distinctions. He describes those things that characterise the forbidden "world"; he calls them "works of the flesh": **"immorality, impurity, licentiousness, idolatry, sorcery, enmity, strife, jealousy, anger, selfishness, dissension, party spirit, envy, drunkenness, carousing, and the like"** (Ga. 5:19-21).

I have met Christians who would not enter a theatre to see a good film or play, because they judge those things "worldly", yet who are shamelessly selfish and greedy; they would disdain a supposedly "worldly" jazz concert, or a symphony, but fail to notice their anger and envy.

They are so proud of their "holy" avoidance of what they mistakenly call "the world" that they never discover how worldly they really are in the scriptural meaning of the term. They strain out gnats but swallow camels. They are latter day Pharisees.

A concert, a book, a meal, a pleasure, an activity, a sport, a relationship, a job, a garment, may all be proper in some settings and improper in others. Any one of those things may sometimes be a focal point for lust or pride, but at other times they may be innocent of guile. To make a blanket rule, "thou shalt not enter a theatre, nor seek public office, nor read a novel, nor wear jewellery, nor watch TV, nor follow a sport, nor eat such foods, nor drink such drinks" (and the like), is not holiness but immature legalism.

Paul gives a better criterion: *"Brethren, whatever is true, whatever is honourable, whatever is just, whatever is pure, whatever is lovely, whatever is gracious, if there is any excellence, if there is anything worthy of praise, think about these things"* (Ph 4:8).

Notice the pronoun "whatever", repeated six times. "Whatever" meets the standards set by the apostle, whether inside or outside the church, is a fit object for Christian contemplation. "Whatever" embodies genuine excellence, "whatever" is praiseworthy, may be confidently pursued.

It seems to me that this all-embracive pronoun banishes completely the false dichotomy many Christians create between the "secular" and the "sacred". That distinction does not exist in scripture. An important group of references reveals a better approach ....

### B) Secular versus sacred?

Many Christians are still imbued with the suspicious fear many ancient philosophers had of the physical world, including natural pleasures and the human body. The biblical authors did not share this aversion -

> *"The earth is the Lord's, and the fullness thereof,*
> *the world and those who dwell therein" (Ps 24:1)*

That statement is typical of the joyful celebration of God's world found everywhere in scripture. There is indeed a "world" that lies in sin; it is the world of corruption, the result of man acting in rebellion. But the larger world remains God's. Our beautiful earth and all its fullness still rests under the divine benediction: "Behold, it is very good" (Ge 1:31). Man is still fulfilling the divine mandate when he goes out into that world, seizes its "fullness", and shapes and subdues it to create his homes, his cities, and his culture (Ge 1:28-30). That ancient mandate is still operative and it is still being honoured by God.

Paul quoted Ps 24:1 in an interesting connection:

> *"Eat whatever is sold in the meat market without raising any question on the ground of conscience; for, 'The earth is the Lord's and everything in it'"* (1 Co. 10:25-26)

It is plain that Paul had not surrendered the earth to the ungodly! Everything in it, except sin, was still God's, and could be received by Christians with thanksgiving.

Paul related that principle specifically to food, but there is no reason to doubt that he would have applied it to any matter about which people had unnecessary scruples. Whatever was sold in the market place of life could be purchased, so long as it conformed to the criteria of truth, honour, justice, purity, loveliness, graciousness, excellence, and worthiness (Ph 4:8). To raise questions on the ground of conscience about such things is to call unholy what God still pronounces holy.

Paul goes on to ask: "Why should my liberty be determined by another man's scruples? If I partake with thankfulness, why am I denounced because of that for which I give thanks?" (vs. 29-30).

Again he is speaking about food, but the principle is readily applied to a wide range of pursuits, activities, and pleasures that more scrupulous souls seek to ban. He concludes: "Whether you eat or drink, **or whatever you do**, do all to the glory of God" (vs. 31).

If the earth and all it contains is the Lord's; if Christians are bidden to receive all things with gladness, including the produce of the land and of the city; if Christians are free to enjoy all that is true and lovely, gracious and excellent, honourable and worthy; then any attempt to distinguish between sacred and secular is misinformed. If these things are all God's, then they are all sacred, whether fashioned by godly or ungodly hands. Fallen humanity obeys God unwittingly, **but it obeys him nonetheless! All that he gives me, by his own hand or by the hand of men, is sanctified by my faith and by my thanksgiving.**

However, Paul does lay down another guideline....

There are things good in themselves, in which I could normally participate freely, but which may sometimes not be expedient or profitable, or which may offend another person -

> *"'All things are lawful,' but not all things are helpful. 'All things are lawful,' but not all things build up. Let no one seek his own good, but the good of his neighbour ... (Many) look after their own interest, not those of Jesus Christ ... 'All things are lawful for me,' but not all things are helpful. 'All things are lawful for me,' but I will not be enslaved by anything" (1 Co 10:23,24; Ph 2:21; 1 Co 6:12).*

Paul is very bold when he writes, "All things are lawful for me." There are not many exclusions there! He takes it for granted that things sinful and corrupt are omitted; but otherwise virtually everything in the world is permitted to him. He has a wonderful liberty of conscience. He is not haunted by gloomy apprehensions of "worldliness"!

But there are some imperatives by which he decides his actions day by day

- will this thing be helpful or deleterious to him; will it promote or hinder his health and true happiness, and especially the interests of Christ; will it tend to build up or cast down?

- will this thing draw him into self-seeking, or will it enlarge his affections toward others and enhance his ability to help them; is it a pleasure simple and innocent, or is it gained at the expense of others; is it a sensible recreation or an act of greedy self-indulgence?

- will this thing strengthen his liberty in Christ, or will it bring him into physical, mental, or spiritual slavery?

- will this thing violate the law of love which obliges him to be careful of his neighbour's feelings and not to cause offence deliberately? In a case such as that he would not so much as eat a plate of meat until the sensitive person was no longer present (1 Co 8:7-13; 10:28-29).

> "All things are yours, whether ... the world or life or death or the present or the future, all are yours; and you are Christ's; and Christ is God's" *(1 Co 3:21-23).*

In connection with the events and opportunities of day by day life, that is one of the most satisfying verses in the Bible. **God has given us his world to enjoy!**

Whatever is a proper part of human experience the Christian should be able to embrace with a pleasure far beyond anything the ungodly know. Nobody should enjoy as Christians can all the pleasures of eating, sleeping, loving, working, playing, giving, receiving - in a word, the real pleasures of life. Above all people, Christians should find happiness in music, literature, art, and all forms of cultural expression. Even death and the unknown future are part of the zest of life for those who recognise them as God's gift.

All things are mine! The ungodly may not realise it; but if they build a great city, they build it for me; if they sing a lovely song, they sing it for me; if they create a noble sculpture, it is designed for my pleasure; if they erect a fine hospital, establish a well-stocked market, set up a just government, invent a useful machine, write a good book, print a truthful newspaper, establish a responsible radio station, send an informative TV picture - whatever they do that is good, **God gives it all to me!**

This is my Father's world; those things are all my Father's creations (though wrought by ungodly men as his unknowing servants); I am free to take from them what I will with thanksgiving and to bring him glory in their use.

Are you not as free as I?

(This study is continued in the next Chapter)

# CHAPTER TWO

# EVERYTHING IS YOURS!

In your previous Chapter we began a study of the Christian's relationship to the world around us, and what Paul meant when he demanded that we "separate" ourselves from the world. The key text was 2 Co 6:14-7:1. Before going any further, you should read that passage again.

We saw what it means to be "separate from sin", and we began to explore also what it means to be "separate from darkness". In particular, we began to examine whether or not there is really any distinction between the "secular" and the "sacred", and what pleasures and things of the "world" are permitted to Christians.

That Chapter concluded in the middle of a discussion on Christian freedom, based on Paul's exciting words: "All things are yours, whether ... the world or life or death or the present or the future, all are yours; and you are Christ's, and Christ is God's" (1 Co 3:21-23). We take up the theme again from there ....

In the wide world of commerce, art, music, literature, sport, education, government, there is comparatively little that the children of God may not employ for their own pleasure or profit - subject always, of course, to the guidelines I have already indicated.

But the point I am stressing is this: very little (when compared with the earth's "fullness") is evil of itself. The Bible allows vastly more than it forbids, despite the attempts of certain ascetic saints to reverse the formula. Such life-denying attempts should be resisted, especially when they take the form of blanket denunciations, or of lists of prohibitions, or of a so-called holiness based on outer conformity to a set of rules, or of a fetter imposed on one man's liberty by another man's scruple. Christ has not so taught us.

Although Paul asserted his care for timid souls who have not yet appropriated this liberty of ours, saying he would not offend them for the world, he still did not hesitate to describe them rather disparagingly as "not possessing this knowledge", as being "weak in faith and in conscience", and as being easily "destroyed." It is not a flattering description! (Ro 14:1-2; 1 Co 8:7-13).

But I hasten to make a distinction between an ascetic who is free in his conscience and one who is bound. The latter person Paul reckons to be immature. The former is simply exercising a God-given right, for it must be recognised that scripture allows either indulgence or abstinence when dealing with the world and the things that are in it. The point is this: whatever is done should be done in freedom of conscience, your own and your brother's. If you choose to indulge you should not condemn your brother for abstaining, and vice versa. Each person has an unequivocal right to determine personally how he or she may best glorify God -

> "Happy is the man who has no reason to condemn himself for what he allows" (Ro 14:22)

> "Let not him who (indulges) despise him who abstains, and let not him who abstains pass judgment on him who (indulges); for God has welcomed him" (vs 3)

> "Who are you to pass judgment on the servant of another? It is before his own Master that he stands or falls" (vs 4)

"One man esteems one day as better than another, while another man esteems all days alike. Let everyone be fully convinced in his own mind" (vs 5).

(For "day" substitute whatever may be at issue: art forms, music styles, literature, involve -ment in social or political life, adornment, dress, "clean" or "unclean" foods, personal habits or behaviour patterns, and the like.)

> *"He who observes the day (etc) observes it in honour of the Lord. He also who eats (etc), eats in honour of the Lord, since he gives thanks to God; while he who abstains, abstains in honour of the Lord, and gives thanks to God ... Why do you pass judgment on your brother? Or you, why do you despise your brother? For we shall all stand before the judgment seat of God ... (and) each of us shall give (personal) account of himself to God" (vs. 10-12)*

> *"I know and am persuaded in the Lord that nothing is unclean in itself; but it is unclean for anyone who thinks it unclean ... He who has doubts is condemned, if he eats (etc.), because he does not act from faith; for whatever does not proceed from faith is sin" (vs 14, 23)*

No one can make these value judgments for you. You and you alone, under the personal guidance of the Holy Spirit, and in harmony with scripture, must decide what is permissible. Whether food or drink, work or play, pleasure or study, music or art, sport or politics, secular or sacred activities, only you can decide what is proper or improper. You should grant to no other person a final right to say, "You cannot play that music, or read that book, or go to that place, or touch that object, or behave in that way, or become involved in that activity."

You may certainly seek another's advice; you may even choose to be directed by him or her; but beware! Do not allow another person's conscience to imprison yours. Do not allow another person to impose his will on you against your own deepest understanding of what God wants you personally to express.

Whatever you do must come out of your own faith, knowing that what you are doing is approved by God, a reflection of your own unique relationship with him, and of the way you can best fulfil all that is his special gift to you. That is the only way you can fully glorify God in your life.

> *"If your brother is being injured by what you eat (etc.), you are no longer walking in love. Do not let what you eat (etc.), cause the ruin of one for whom Christ died. So do not let what is good to you be spoken of as evil ... Let us then pursue what makes for peace and for mutual upbuilding ... Everything is indeed clean, but it is wrong for anyone to make others fall by what he eats (etc.)" (vs. 15-21)*

In conformity with that instruction, we should neither impose our personal taboos on others, nor ignore their taboos when we are in their company. Sympathetic concern for each other is expected by Christ. To each man his own inhibitions, mores, and restraints; but from each man also, love that makes him tender toward his neighbour's sensibilities!

> *"It is right not to eat meat or drink wine or do anything that makes your brother stumble or be upset or be weakened. The faith that you have, keep between yourself and God" (vs. 21-22)*

I can do anything my faith allows me, and this faith is formed by my knowledge of scripture, of myself (my strengths and weakness, my positives and negatives), and of the will of God for my life - that is, how God has called me to glorify him.

Such faith cannot be discovered frivolously. It requires honesty and freedom from prejudice. To know yourself, to have a sober and true appraisal of yourself (Ro 12:3), is often difficult to achieve. But you cannot come to a place of inner harmony, of peace, and of stability in your Christian walk until you do make this discovery. God is willing to assist you, so long as you are genuinely willing to put aside all preconceptions and earnestly listen to him -

> *"If any of you lacks wisdom, let him ask God, who gives to all men generously and without reproaching, and it will be given him" (Ja 1:5-8)*

But when you come to that faith you will almost certainly find that God allows you things he forbids others, and forbids you things he allows to others. So keep your faith between yourself and God. Where you have **liberty**, rejoice in it privately, lest you grieve those who cannot share your freedom. Where you are **restricted**, obey silently, lest you hinder those who are not bound, and so prevent them from rendering their own unique thanks to God.

On this matter of our freedom to indulge or abstain, and on our responsibility toward each other, see again 1 Co 8:7-13; 9:1, 3-5, 12-14, 19-23; 10:24, 27-11:1.

> *"God richly furnishes us with everything to enjoy"*
> *(1 Ti 6:17)*

Our task is to dwell among this bounty, wisely selecting from it whatever is helpful, profitable, and beneficial to ourselves, our neighbour, and above all, to our service to God.

Now you should realise that the criteria I have given might lead you to a novel as readily as to the Bible; or they might take you to a party as well as to prayer, or to a concert as well as to a hymn, or to a film as well as to a sermon, or to home as well as to church, or to sport as well as to fasting, or to serve God through the "secular" as well as through the "sacred" - **for to the child of God all things are sacred; they all bear the insignia "Holy to the Lord"** (Zc 14:20-21).

The man who genuinely believes that "nothing is unclean of itself" has an advantage here. It is easier for him to accept the validity of the ascetic view, than it is for an ascetic to look with favour on things that to him are distasteful. Christians with an ascetic disposition may find the idea of freedom impossible to accept. They may be disposed to quote some supposedly anti-pleasure texts, such as Pr 21:17; Lu 8:14; Tit 3:3; 2 Ti 3:4; 1Jn 2:15; Ja 4:4. Passages like those have often been used as a basis for opposition to all so-called physical or secular pleasures, as distinct from so-called spiritual or sacred pleasures. But that kind of religious kill-joyism is not endorsed by scripture. Apart from passages already quoted above, consider the following -

> *"I know that there is nothing better for them than to be happy and enjoy themselves as long as they live; also that it is God's gift to man that everyone should eat and drink and take pleasure in all his toil ... Now the Spirit expressly says that in later times some will depart from the faith ... who forbid marriage and enjoin abstinence from foods (etc.) which God created to be received with thanksgiving by those who believe and know the truth. For everything created by God is good, and nothing is to be rejected if it is received with thanksgiving; for then it is consecrated by the word of God and prayer ... To the pure all things are pure" (Ec 3:12,13; 1Ti 4:4; Tit 1:15).*

However, since the Epicureans first promulgated the philosophy, "Eat, drink, and be merry, for tomorrow we die," **Christians who have misunderstood both the philosophy and the scriptures have damned as carnal all physical and sensual pleasure**. But that is throwing out the table cloth with the bread crumbs. It lacks discrimination, and it betrays a shallow perception of values.

Be wary then of those structured souls who quote with accusation the vain word of the rich man, "Take your ease, eat, drink, and be merry" (Lu 12:19), yet fail to approve the joyful celebration of the prodigal's father, "Bring the fatted calf and kill it, and let us eat and make merry" (15:23).

The indictment of the rich man was not that he made merry, nor that he was wealthy, but that he was not "rich toward God" (12:21). A godly man will be equally content with wealth or poverty, according to the Father's disposition of his life, for his real treasure is in heaven (vs. 22-34).

No doubt it is true for the ungodly that all of their eating and drinking and merriment is ashes in the mouth, for they have no goal but death nor any destiny but the grave (1 Co 15:32). But we who have conquered death in Christ are not so! We are at ease in our souls! At the right hand of our God there are pleasures for evermore - pleasures of which all the happiness of this present life is but a sweet foretaste! (Jb 36:10-11; Ps 16:11).

Norman Geisler writes:

> "Real pleasure is not found by separating certain external acts and spheres from others and labelling them good or evil. It is found only as one receives everything, the physical world included, as a gift from God. **The enjoyments of life are all gifts of God to be received, not evils to be avoided. But one cannot be happy by clinging to the gift and neglecting the giver. Things are not an end in**

**themselves; they are a means to the end. Satisfaction is found in God alone**. As Jesus said, 'A man's life does not consist in the abundance of his possessions' (Lu 12:15).

"One cannot truly enjoy the good things of life unless they are subordinated to God. 'Seek first God's Kingdom and his righteousness,' said Jesus, 'and all these things shall be yours as well' (Mt 6:33). Those who worship and serve the creature rather than the Creator cannot be blessed of God (Ro 1:25). Solomon wrote, 'Every man also to whom God has given wealth and possessions and power to enjoy them ... this is the gift of God' (Ec 5:19). True pleasure is found not in things as such but in things as gifts from God. **Without the recognition that temporal pleasures are from God and that eternal pleasure is found only in God, there is no true satisfaction.**

"The hedonist's problem is that he seeks to find eternal happiness **in** a temporal world rather than **through** it and **from** God. He vainly attempts to fill an infinite capacity for satisfaction with finite things. As St. Augustine noted long ago, 'The heart is restless until it finds its rest in God.' "[4]

To sum up: the rule that should govern our relationships with the world and the things that are in it is **epieikeia** - "sweet reasonableness". As the ancient Preacher said: **"For everything there is a season, and a time for every matter under**

---

[4]  From an article, **The Christian As Pleasure – Seeker**, in Christianity Today, September 26, 1975, pg 11.

**heaven ... God has made everything beautiful in
its time**" (see Ec 3:1-13).

Knowing what is the right way to do the right thing
in the right place at the right time - that is true
wisdom and grace.

## 1. <u>Separate From False Religion</u>

"What accord does Christ have with Belial?"

"Belial" was a kind of derogatory personal name for the devil. It
means "utterly worthless" - a good description of that base fiend! It
was also used as a synonym for false religions, which were thought
to be inspired by Satan.

There are several aspects of false religion of which you should be
aware. The presence of one or more of these aspects indicates that
the cult is either non-Christian, or represents a warped form of
Christianity.

A) Some Christians build their confidence in the gospel
entirely on their personal experience of it - that is, they insist that
the gospel must be true because of the inner peace and joy, the
personal satisfaction, their belief in Christ has brought them. Their
testimony is no doubt true. But that kind of emotional response to
faith is not unique to Christianity. Devotees of other religions
often present similar testimonies, and their witness is frequently no

less enthusiastic than that of most zealous Christians.[5] A genuine presentation of the Christian religion, while it may reflect the love, joy, and peace which faith in Christ certainly brings, will concentrate mainly on –

the <u>total satisfaction</u> the gospel gives, not just to our need for an emotional response to God, but to every aspiration for moral renewal, for spiritual enlightenment, for forensic innocence, for intellectual harmony, for physical security, and for eternal life.

the complete consistency and reasonableness of the Christian world-view, in contrast with the cosmogonies of other faiths, which frequently require an abandonment of good sense and rational thought, and a blind acceptance of dogma without substance. Whether or not the Christian world-view is accepted as true, it must still be acknowledged to be internally consistent, to be essentially rational, and to be lacking in the absurdities which bedevil the cults.

the manner in which the gospel relates harmoniously to all that man sees, hears, feels, in daily life. The gospel fits comfortably into the whole human experience. There is nothing in the gospel which is counter to what man has experienced of himself and the world in which he lives. The gospel does contain divine revelation, which no man could have discovered by searching for it, and which comes as a gift from God, but this revelation is recognised as truth (or at least, as potentially true) because it is seen to be harmonious with life and reason. There is no inherent absurdity or self-contradiction in the gospel, nothing that must be at once categorised as irrational and as

---

[5]    For example, here is how a follower of the Krishna Consciousness movement describes the benefits he has obtained from belief in his Hindu deity. The extracts are from a letter to the swami who first introduced him to Krishna: "Every moment of those precious few moments I had with you is inscribed in my mind... You have given me a new vision, new concepts of life... As a matter of fact, you have given me a new birth, and I have now become a true 'dvija' (twice born person)... I feel like I was a beggar on the street and all of a sudden the all-merciful Lord made me a billionaire overnight..." (**Back to Godhead** magazine, # 51, 1973, page 19). Similar testimonies can be found in the publications of most cults.

inconsistent with life and good order. Even those who reject the gospel are constrained to admit that, when taken on its own terms, it does present a view of the world which provides a balanced answer to the dilemmas of existence, morality, and destiny. The world-view presented by many of the cults requires an abnegation of reason and the adoption of beliefs which gain no support from history or life.

So then, we say that confidence in the Christian world-view is based on: its basic reasonableness; the demonstrable authenticity of the Bible; the actions of God in history; the life, death, and resurrection of Christ; and only lastly on the benefits it brings to its adherents. The cults major on experience; the gospel majors on revelation and reason.

B) Certain emphases are common to most cults, and expose them as presenting an ethic or a dogma which diverges from the Christian view. These false emphases fall into four major categories –

     i.   pantheism/transcendentalism

Pantheism and transcendentalism are opposite extremes.

Pantheism holds that God and the physical universe are indistinguishable, that God does not exist as a separate personality, but is rather the expression of the physical forces of nature.

Transcendentalism holds that God is so glorious and holy that he disdains to take any notice of puny man, and that it is foolish to think of God as being actively involved in human affairs.

A great many cults are drawn irresistibly toward one of those extreme views. By contrast, Christianity is unique in the remarkable way it has succeeded in blending the two ideas, of the imminence and the transcendence of God.

## ii. asceticism

As I have already indicated, an ascetic viewpoint, when it is extreme and legalistic, and particularly when it is made a matter of righteousness (Col 2:20-23), must be seen as a foreign importation into the gospel. But it is common for people who have not learned how to receive righteousness as a gift of God through Christ to work hard to achieve their own righteousness by self-mortification.

But any offer of salvation through asceticism must be rejected by Christians as heresy.

## iii. nihilism

This is a view which either denies all objective existence to the world and to man; or it may seek to destroy all self-awareness under an overwhelming consciousness of God; or it may even seek to lose all personal identity through merger with the Divine.

But it is anti-Christian to teach that self-annihilation is the pathway to the discovery of God. The gospel does not say that to find God is to lose yourself. On the contrary, we are invited by the scriptures to enter into a relationship with God through Christ that actually enables us to find ourselves for the first time. Knowledge of God does not obscure my knowledge of myself; rather, ignorance and blindness are removed, and now I know myself and am aware of myself as never before!

## iv. irrationalism

There is an inescapable irrationalism underlying the beliefs of all cults. Many of them, however, manage to obscure that irrationalism by demanding from their devotees adherence to strict ritual observances. Form takes the place of substance. Incantations, ceremonies, chants, repetitive prayers, are substituted for a coherent, consistent, reasonable view of life.

But one of the basic invitations in scripture is: "Come, let us reason together, says the Lord." Any form of belief that requires the sacrifices of intelligence on the altar of ritual cannot represent the gospel. Any religious system that requires reason to prostitute itself to dogma bolstered by ceremony cannot be called Christian.

C) There are certain other aspects of doctrine or practice that commonly identify a Christian deviation, or a false cult. These may be listed as –

i. any religion which does not name Christ as Lord and as the only source of salvation and of eternal life.

ii. any form of occultism, spiritualism, necromancy, and the like (Is 8:19-20; Le 19:31; De 18:10-14; etc.)

iii. cults which call themselves "Christian" while denying some of the tenets of the gospel (2 Ti 4:3-4; 3:8-9; Ga 1:6-9; 2 Co 11:3-4; etc.)

iv. those who hold to a correct form of godliness, but who have entirely lost its power, making their profession a sham. Paul is emphatic: "Avoid such people" (2 Ti 3:5)

D) Separate In Faith

*"Do not be mismated with unbelievers ... (for) what does a believer have in common with an un-believer?"*

That passage is often used to dissuade Christians from marrying unconverted persons, or from becoming involved in business partnerships with unbelievers. No doubt that is a good dissuasion. The scriptures elsewhere decree that a Christian should marry only someone who is "in the Lord", and it is probably wise for Christians to avoid as much as possible being "unequally yoked together" (lit.) with non-Christians.

But applying the text in this way misses its real meaning. If this passage is actually intended to prevent Christians from entering into contractual arrangements with non-Christians, then we face insurmountable difficulties, for we are all dependent every day upon unbelievers for the things we need to sustain life and health. All believers are obliged to relate closely to unbelievers in home, office, shop, factory, neighbourhood, bank, school, entertainment, government - indeed, almost everywhere. It is not possible for us to avoid this close involvement with, and daily dependency upon, unbelievers.

Plainly, then, Paul's prohibition cannot be directed against ordinary commercial alliances, nor against social intercourse, public involvement, and community activities. After all, Paul did not say, "do not be yoked" to unbelievers, but "do not be unequally yoked." The emphasis should be placed on "unequally", not on "yoked".

In what sense, then, are we who believe to avoid being wrongfully mated with unbelievers? Surely the real demand is for Christians to separate themselves from the way the world **"believes".** The contrast is not between godly and ungodly, but between belief and unbelief: "do not be unequally yoked with **unbelievers."**

The distinction between the two groups is the kind of faith that characterises them; their attitudes are more important than their life styles; their goals and aspirations are more significant than their immediate behaviour; the determinant factor in the separation of the two groups, the cause of the unbridgeable hiatus between them, is the utter disparity in their value systems. Other barriers are surmountable, but this is impenetrable. Their **"yoke"** and ours remain utterly disparate, completely irreconcilable.

What are these incompatible "yokes"?

## The "Yoke" Of The Unbeliever

## The "Yoke" Of The Believer

His only treasure is located on this earth, in material possessions. He has no other wealth, so he devotes his whole life to amassing possessions and he clings to them fiercely. His money is his only security, he depends on it for everything. His happiness is bound up with earthly things, hence it is always at risk, and he lives in anxiety, always apprehensive that he will lose what he has gained.

His treasure is in heaven, in the kingdom prepared for him by the Father. He is content to enjoy whatever worldly goods the Father may enable him to gather (in fact he can enjoy them more richly than the unbeliever), but he is cheerfully willing, if God requires it, to sell all that he has, give it to the poor, and to follow his Lord to the ends of the earth. He keeps a light touch on everything material, because his real security is in God, and his happiness is to do God's will.

For him the ultimate disaster is death; the grave is an unspeakable obscenity, a mocker of all his pretensions, the destroyer of all his dreams, the abandonment of all his hopes, a rottenness beneath his feet, the prostration of all his dignity.

For him death has no terror; and the grave is not an end but a glorious beginning, the door through which he steps into paradise, an entrance to eternal bliss, the step by which he climbs into God's immediate presence and by which he gains the realisation of his deepest desires.

He is unable to discover pleasure in any source save the physical, hence his pleasures remain locked into time, space,

He richly enjoys his Father's world, and all that is in it, but his chief delight is found not in physical but in spiritual and the material world; he is easily satiated but never satisfied; and like a dog is driven back to his own vomit, and to wallowing like a sow in the mire (2 Pe 2:22).

pleasures; such never bring weariness in their use, nor do they sicken and enervate, nor do they exhaust or destroy; rather they cause the participant to rise constantly from glory to glory, in paeans of praise and gladness (2 Co 3:18).

For him, prayer is arrant folly, nothing seems to him more futile; it offends his pride and carnal self-sufficiency; it defies his natural logic and mocks his earth-bound philosophy; he cannot conceive the possibility of divine intervention in human affairs.

His greatest resource is prayer; he shrinks from depending solely on human wisdom and natural skills; he puts no final trust in the flesh and its ways, but seeks to live on a spiritual plane where he has access to heaven's limitless assets and God's loving guidance.

He looks on Christians as fools who are soon parted from their money; he can see no reason nor sense in giving money or time to the church; he thinks that Christians pay dearly and stupidly for their few hours of religious entertainment; the concept of tithing seems to him to be especially inane; it probably offends him more, and is more incomprehensible to him, than any other aspect of Christian life.

He delights in giving above getting, and thinks of all his gifts as a small return for the bounty the Lord has showered upon him; he also looks on his giving as an investment in the future, it is capital he is laying down towards his inheritance in the kingdom of God; he believes that by God's favour he will prosper more in the use of what remains after he has given than he would have done if he had retained all for himself; he thinks the tithe is a reasonable basis for giving and tends to increase rather than decrease it; he believes the promise of God.

I see this, then as the meaning of the injunction for believers not to be unequally yoked together with unbelievers. We are to divorce ourselves totally from the **naturalism** of the unbeliever, and to espouse ourselves boldly to Christ, being determined to maintain our identity as the **supernatural** children of God.

As Shadrach, Meshach and Abednego walked in the midst of the flames, without even the smell of smoke fouling their garments, so we can live in an unbelieving world yet remain untouched by its attitudes and ways.

We are called to show a separation of **spirit and of belief. We are not required to isolate ourselves physically and socially,** but we are required to be a people apart in ambition, affection, and assurance. Our confidence has a different base, our lives have a different direction, our joy has a different source, our love has a different motive, our security has a different defence, and our hope has a different guarantee.

### E) <u>Separate In Worship</u>

*"What agreement does the temple of God have with idols?"*

If you want to make an enemy of a man, there is a sure way to do it: take a stick and shatter his idol. People cling to their gods tenaciously. They will surrender all they possess before they will let go of their gods. Whatever deity a man worships is to him the most important thing in his life - he will usually defend it with his life.

If you doubt the truth of those assertions consider what would happen if you visited Thailand as a tourist, became disgusted by the sight of a bloated Buddha squatting in his temple, seized the idol, threw it outside, and smashed it to pieces? What do you think the worshippers would do to you? Touch a man's idol and you touch him! Hurt his god and you will arouse him to a frenzy!

For this reason the world hates us: we scorn its idols, we mock its golden gods, we laugh at its graven images, we deride its absurd deities.

The gods of this world are

     i.   Materialism. The world worships the idol of natural wealth and possessions. But we know that God has appointed a day when he will "shake not only the earth but also the heaven ... (which) indicates the removal of what is shaken, as of what has been made, in order that that cannot be shaken may remain. Therefore let us offer to God acceptable worship with reverence and awe; for our God is a consuming fire" (He 12:26-29).

In that day the materialistic idols of this world, and the pedestals on which they stand, will alike crumble to dust and vanish for ever (1:10-12). But our God remains. The city he has built for us has foundations that can never be moved (11:10, 17-16). Those who know these things can never be captivated by this world's ashen gods, nor can their souls be enslaved by idol worship.

     ii.   Power. The world worships power. It craves to conquer by force and rule by command. But we mock its feeble pretensions. We who believe possess an invincible faith ( 1 Jn 5:4), we belong to an indestructible church (Mt 16:18), we are indwelt by an unconquerable Spirit (Ep 3:16), and we worship an immutable Christ (He 13:8).

Since we serve him who claims "all power" for himself (Mt 28:18) we can easily disdain the pretended strength of this world's gods.

iii. <u>Selfishness</u>. The doctrine of the world's deity is summed up in one word: "get". By contrast, the doctrine of Christ is "give". Between those two concepts there can be no reconciliation.

If the emphasis of your life is personal gain, then you are of the world, worldly; but if your desire is the gain of others, then you are of God, godly. In the end, only givers gain. Those whose motivation is to get will find that they lose: "One man gives freely, yet grows all the richer; another withholds what he should give, and only suffers want. A liberal man will be enriched, and one who waters will himself be watered" (Pr 11:24-25; see also Mt 16:24-27).

iv. <u>Hate</u>. The world reserves to itself the right to hate; but we Christians accept that we have only one right and one duty: love. Not only do we accept this but we affirm that love is ultimately stronger than hate. He who hates will be ruined by his own malice; but he who loves will triumph over every foe. Nothing can finally destroy those who are resolute in love, for love engulfs all its enemies.

The world prostrates itself before the vicious god of hate; but we spurn this hideous deity, and worship the living God, whose sweetest attribute is this: he is love (1 Jn 4:7-8).

So we are called to separate ourselves from the idols this world adores. We can have no part of their gods. We abhor and abjure their deities. And we achieve this separation by allying ourselves, says Paul, with "the temple of God" - that is, by staying close together as a worshipping company of people who gather to hear the voice of the true God and to be instructed in righteousness. We are as those of old were, who "devoted themselves to the apostles' teaching and fellowship, to the breaking of bread and prayers ... (who) distributed to them all, as any had need, and (who) day by day attended the temple together ... with glad and generous hearts, praising God" (Ac 2:42-47).

# CONCLUSION

Now we have examined five aspects of Christian separation -

> from sin
> from the world
> from false religion
> from unbelievers
> from idols.

We have also seen the marvellous promise God gives to those who so separate themselves -

> to live with them
> to move among them
> to be their God
> to be a Father to them
> to welcome them.

These things being so, Paul brings it all to a good conclusion -

> *"Since we have these promises beloved, let us cleanse ourselves from every defilement of body and spirit, and make holiness perfect in the fear of God"*
> *(2 Co 7:1).*

But remember the two maxims I set before you at the beginning of these chapters. They do not tell you what decisions to make, but they do expose the principles on which to make those decisions that are right for you.

### The first maxim is

♦ allow yourself only what you can do without personal recrimination (Ro 14:22).

### The second maxim is

♦ be governed by sweet reasonableness, that gracious attribute expressed in the noun *epieikeia* (Ph 4:5).

If you are happy in what you allow yourself, if you have learned to handle the world with gracious moderation, then you will have made a good start to living successfully as a Christian.

# CHAPTER THREE

# THE FOUR LOVES

The previous Chapter applied the lovely idea of *epieikeia* to God's world and to your attitude to it. In this Chapter and the next I want to apply the same idea to your attitude toward yourself and the people around you. My intention is to demonstrate the kind of inner poise that should characterise a Christian's social relationships. This will lay a foundation for the topics discussed in the next Section, "Living With Your Neighbour."

But first, look again at that remarkable Christian grace that we began to explore in the first Chapter: the grace of *epieikeia*. This word does not occur in the NT as often as might be expected - but perhaps that is because it already had a long and honoured history in Greek ethical writings, and the attributes it expresses were widely considered to be an essential part of civilised human relationships. The ideal portrayed by *epieikeia*, although it was infrequently realised, was already embedded in Greek and Roman society.

But Christ has made the ideal real. Through the grace he imparts, it is possible for all of our relationships to be marked by all that *epieikeia* signifies.

I mentioned at the beginning of the first Chapter that *epieikeia* occurs seven times in the NT (four times as an adjective, once as a substantive noun, and twice as a noun.) Perhaps the number seven, the number of perfection in scripture, itself indicates the great value of this Christian grace!

**Those seven occurrences are -**

1.  Tertullus, when accusing Paul to the Roman governor Felix said, "I beg you in your *epieikeia* to hear us briefly" (Ac 24:4).

2.  Paul, wishing to exemplify *epieikeia* in his ministry to the Corinthians, and wishing them to display the same grace, pointed to Christ as its source: "I entreat you, by the meekness and *epieikeia* of Christ ... " (2 Co 10:1).

3.  *"Let your epieikeia[6] be known to all men" (Ph 4:5).*

4.  *"A bishop must be above reproach ... not violent but epieikes" (1 Ti 3:2,3).*

5.  Paul instructed Titus to remind all the Christians "to speak evil of no one, to avoid quarrelling, to be *epieikes,* and **to show perfect courtesy toward all men"** (Tit 3:2).

6.  *"The wisdom from above is first pure, then peaceable, then epieikes, open to reason, full of mercy and good fruits, without uncertainty or insincerity" (Ja 3:17).*

7.  *Servants are instructed to "be submissive to (their) masters with all respect, not only to the kind and epieikes, but also to the overbearing" (1 Pe 2:18).*

In those references *epieikeia* is sometimes found in contrasting, and sometimes in complementary settings. But together they convey what *epieikeia* represents: **a sense of moderation, graciousness, and fairminded behaviour suitably adapted to each occasion.**

---

[6]   The Greek text here uses the substantive form of the adjective, name, to epiekes

This grace is contrasted with injustice, indifference, arrogance, derision, violence, evil speaking, quarrelling, discourtesy, and rebellion.

But it is coupled with justice, kindness, gentleness, peaceableness, courtesy, reasonableness, and mercy.

Those are the attributes we should be known for in our dealings with all men, including ourselves.

This Chapter and the next will explore these things.

## LOVING YOUR NEIGHBOUR

I have shown you (in the first two Chapters) that there are two extremes in the way many people relate to the world; there are also two extremes in the way people relate to their neighbours; they tend either to idolise or to **enslave each other.**

At both extremes the name of the game is exploitation. Those who press their neighbours under domination, or who exalt their neighbours into divinity, are both guilty of using other people for their own selfish gratification.

Some people have a slave mentality and wish to be tyrannised; others have a despotic urge, and seek to tyrannise - but the Christian should seek neither to be lord nor serf. We are enjoined rather to serve each other lovingly as brothers, showing perfect courtesy and consideration to all.

Even when rebuke is called for, when discipline must be administered, or a penalty exacted, our actions should never reflect vengeance or malice, but fair-minded restraint, and tempered justice.

## 1. Christ Our Example

Paul uses two surprising nouns to describe the nature of Jesus. I say "surprising" because of the true identity of Christ. Is he not "the Lord of glory" - he who has "all power in heaven and on earth", in whom and for whom "all things were created, visible and invisible, whether thrones or dominions or principalities or authorities?" (Col 1:16). Yet Paul describes him as "meek" *(prautes*) and "gentle" *(epieikeia)* (2 Co 10:1).

Meek? Gentle?

How incongruous those expressions seem when they are applied to him in whom dwells all the fullness of the Godhead! "Regal" and "Irresistible", or "Almighty" and "Terrible", would seem to be more appropriate descriptions!

But Christ has chosen to ally himself with meekness rather than majesty, and with gentleness rather than grandeur. So he has become the perfect example of all that *epieikeia* **signifies.**

So then, when scripture demands that all men should know us by our *epieikeia*, it is saying only that we should follow the example of our Lord and Saviour. As he walked, so are we to walk. As he is, so are we to be.

But Christ is willing to be more than our example. He is also our source. Not only has he shown us the pattern of *epieikeia*, he is also the provider of this grace, as he is of all others. Without a conscious union with him, a deliberate surrender to his will, and an eager appropriation by faith, we cannot possess this nor any other Christian grace.

Your *epieikeia* will be known to all men when you resolve that it shall be so, and when you set yourself to so walk in faith with Christ that he is steadily able to build into you more and more of his beauty.

## 2. Love In Action

I have been speaking as though this sweet reasonableness, this gentle forbearance, this gracious moderation which is *epieikeia* were the chief Christian grace. It is not, of course, for that honour is reserved for another noun: **love**. But *epieikeia* **expresses love in action, love tempering and guiding our social relationships;** it describes the kind of attitude and behaviour love should produce. If we love in Christ, then we should walk and talk among our fellows with gracious moderation.

It will be profitable now, since love is the deep foundation of every Christian virtue, including *epieikeia,* and the true motivation in all Christian relationships, to explore this new theme.

Paul wrote: "Let love be genuine" (Ro 12:9). To love genuinely, is to love the right person, in the right way, at the right time. What that means can be seen in the four different words the Greeks used to express love.

In this respect Greek is richer and more precise than English. When it moves away from "love" English has to depend on words that are much weaker - such as "liking", "fondness", "affection", "friendship". Hence we tend to use the one word "love" to embrace an amazing variety of situations and relationships - from the most profound to the most profane.

But the Greeks had a clearer concept of the four different kinds of love, and of the appropriate setting for each of them. Without this insight, one person may love another in the wrong way, and thus harm them both.

The four kinds of love are -

## A) *EROS* - Sensual Love

*Eros* does not occur in the NT, perhaps because in the Greek world it had become rather debased, and tended to have overtones of immorality and fornication. Basically, however, **eros describes the deep, passionate, sensual love that can exist between a man and a woman.**

Within a Christian setting *eros* is permitted only between man and wife; but in that relationship it is completely proper and wholly desirable. Erotic pleasure within marriage is a gift of God, and it may be freely explored in all of its dimensions, and all of its pleasures may be tasted and enjoyed.

*Eros* is beautifully depicted in The Song of Solomon, which is essentially a series of poems in praise of erotic love. The delights of marital intercourse are also eulogised or approved in: Ge 2:23, 24; 26:8; De 24:5; Ps 45; Pr 5:15-19; Is 62:5; 1 Co 7:3-4; He 13:4. A man and his wife should feel free to be ravished by each other's love, to abandon themselves to each other in *eros*, and to give to each other and receive from each other all the happiness their passion can arouse.

But, for a Christian, *eros* outside of marriage (except as a developing thing in courtship) is strictly forbidden. No wife may dare to look at a man other than her husband with *eros*. Nor may a man or a woman look at another of the same sex with *eros*. Nor may a father hold *eros* toward his daughter, nor a sister toward her brother, nor a mother toward her son.

In fact, any expression of *eros* outside of the framework of marriage is marked by scripture as vicious sin, which will surely attract a divine penalty.

The reason for this severe stricture against illicit *eros* lies in its nature as one of the deepest, most primeval life-forces within man. **To ignore the strong restraint placed on *eros* by the law of God is to tear at the vitals of your own being.** The penalty for undisciplined *eros* is harsh and inescapable, not only for the individual, but also for society. A community that allows unfettered expressions of *eros*, that endorses illicit sexual relations, that laughs at the biblical categories of immorality, is damning itself. It is battering mindlessly at its own soul, and savagely eroding its own foundations. No society that has allowed the sexual energies of its people to run wild, or that has encouraged unbridled sensuality, has ever survived in strength. A kind of creeping self-disgust, a sad ennui, a death wish, has always finally overtaken *eros* **abusers.**

There are a multitude of biblical references declaring that *eros* may be freely expressed only within marriage; and even then it must remain subject to the laws of mutual respect, of tenderness, and of restraint (in a word, *epieikeia*).

But one reference in particular highlights the strictness with which Christ viewed this matter -

> *"You have heard that it was said, 'You shall not commit adultery.' But I say to you that every one who looks at a woman lustfully has already committed adultery with her in his heart. If your right eye causes you to sin, pluck it out and throw it away; it is better that you lose one of your members than that your whole body be thrown into hell. And if your right hand causes you to sin, cut it off and throw it away; it is better that you lose one of your members than that your whole body go into hell"* (Mt 5:27-30).

You would be better off to maim yourself than to offend the law of God that governs *eros*! But fortunately Christ himself has provided us with a spiritual method of achieving the same effect. We are told that we can actually put to death whatever in us violates God's will, excising it by faith. This is a better method by far - reaching deeper than mere physical mutilation - and permanently effective! See Ro 6:11-14; Ep 4:20-23; Col 3:1-5, 12-16: etc.

Nonetheless, the violence of Jesus' saying ("pluck out your eye, cut off your hand") is a stern warning of the penalty violated *eros* will exact; and it is also a graphic indication of the extent to which our health and happiness is involved with *eros* **rightly used.**

The laws of God are neither capricious nor arbitrary. If Christ asserts that it were better to be blind than to have a fornicating eye, he does so, not to impose a gloomy bondage on human pleasure, but because he understands the deep integration of *eros* with the very fibre of our being. He knows that erotic licence will eventually bring man a sorrow far more bitter than amputation or blindness. He would spare you that pain.

But let me say it again: within marriage, and especially within Christian marriage, husband and wife may find the utmost delight in each others' bodies, and they are given liberty by God to explore whatever pathway of erotic pleasure they mutually desire and rejoice in.

### B) *STORGE* - Family Love

*Storge* (pronounced "storgay") was the word used by the Greeks to describe family affection. It expressed in particular the fondness of parents for their children, and of children for their parents, and for each other.

*Storge* as a noun is not found in the NT. In fact it occurs only once, in the form of a kindred adjective, **philostorgos** = tenderly affectionate. This single occurrence is in Ro 12:10, which reads literally: "In brotherly love to one another **loving warmly**."

Here is what some commentators say about this passage, which implies that the Christian community is not merely a **society**, but a loving family -

> "We must be affectionate to one another in brotherly love. The word Paul uses for affectionate is 'philostorgos', and 'storge' is the Greek word for **family love**. We must love each other, because we are members of one family. We are not strangers to each other within the Christian Church; much less are we isolated units; we are brothers and sisters of each other, because we have the one Father, even God. The Christian Church is not a collection of acquaintances; it is not even a gathering of friends; it is a family in God."[7]

> "(Paul selected an adjective based on **storge** to intimate that the Christians form one family)." (Bengel)

> "The word used here occurs nowhere else in the NT. It properly denotes tender affection, such as that which subsists between parents and children; and it means, that Christians should have similar feelings towards each other, as belonging to the same family, and as united in the same principles and interests."[8]

---

[7]  William Barclay, **The Daily Study Bible**, "Romans", pg.177  The Saint Andrews Press, Edinburgh. 1962

[8]  William Barclay, **The Daily Study Bible**, "Romans", pg.177.  The Saint Andrews Press, Edinburgh. 1962

"(**Philostorgos**) signifies not only love, but a readiness and inclination to love, the most genuine and free affection, kindness flowing out as from a spring. It properly denotes the love of parents to their children, which, as it is the most tender, so it is the most natural of any, unforced, unconstrained; such must our love be to one another, and such it will be where there is greatest courtesy and obligingness that may be ... And what can be sweeter on this side of heaven than to love and be beloved? He that thus watereth shall be watered also himself."[9]

## C) *PHILIA* - Friendly Love

*Philia* represents the love of deep friendship. It has the sense of an earnest attachment to someone or something. It is full of warmth and affection. A kindred noun *philema* means "a kiss" - "Greet one another with a holy kiss" ... "Greet one another with the kiss of love" (Ro 16:16; 1 Co 16:20; 2 Co 13:12; 1 Th 5:26; 1 Pe 5:14). A kindred verb, *phileo*, is used some twenty-five times in the NT, in a variety of settings, but all of them conveying a sense of intense love, fondness, or desire. Hence Jesus spoke of those who love father or mother more than him (Mt 10:37); there are those who love the place of honour at feasts (23:6); the Father loves the Son (Jn 5:20); Jesus loved Lazarus (11:3, 36); there are those who love life too much (12:25); the Father loved the disciples because they loved Jesus (16:27); if we do not love the Lord then we are under a curse (1 Co 16:22).

*Philia* itself occurs only once in the NT: "Ungrateful creatures! Do you not know that **friendship** with the world is **enmity** with God?" (Ja 4:4). This contrast with "enmity" indicates the intensity *philia* can carry.

---

[9] **Matthew Henry's Commentary**, vol 6, "Acts to Revelation", pg. 461. Marshal, Morgan, and Scott, London, 1953

Another noun akin to *philia* is **philos**, which is commonly translated as "friend" (some thirty times). **Philos** means someone (or something) who is very dear to one's affections. It is found in Jn 15:13: "Greater love has no man than this, that a man lay down his life for his **friends**." It is also found in 3 Jn 15: "The **friends** greet you. Greet the **friends**, every one of them." It is evident that Christians are presumed to have *philia* for each other.

**Philia**, then, in a Christian setting, may be said to express two things –

the warm friendship and affection, the delight in each other's company, the joy of fellowship, that all Christians should share with each other

the deeper attachment that belongs to special friendship - and this is a more proper use of the word. At its heart, *philia* expresses an intensity of emotion that surpasses the idea of casual or everyday friendship. This depth of feeling, as I have already indicated, is shown by the way *philia* is contrasted with hate, and by the way it is linked with a kiss, and with the supreme sacrifice one friend can make for another.

Christian love, then, should consist of a strong and fervent attachment, of friendship that forges a powerful bond. This is shown further by the way the Greeks linked **philia** with other nouns to form intensified compound nouns -

| | | |
|---|---|---|
| *philagathos* | - | lover of goodness (fostering virtue) |
| *philadelphos* | - | brother-loving |
| *philandros* | - | husband-loving |
| *philanthropos* | - | mankind-loving (benevolence) |
| *philarguros* | - | lover of money |
| *philedonos* | - | lover of pleasure |
| *philotheos* | - | lover of God |
| | - | and many others. |

In each case there is a sense of the kind of love that binds a lover to the object of his affections. In this sense *philia* is a stronger word than *storge*. Hence, a father may have *storge* for all of his children, but *philia* for only one; or a man may have *storge* for a group of his friends, but *philia* for only some of them. Thus David loved Jonathon above all his friends; and among the twelve disciples, Jesus loved especially Peter, James, and John; and even among these three, he loved John the more (cp. Jn 20:2).

So in the family, in the church, we may (and should) have *storge* for every member, but *philia* (in its deepest sense) for only a few.

This brings me to a problem that has grieved many sincere people of God. It sometimes happens in the church, or in life, that a man and woman who are already married will meet, become friends, and then discover that their friendship is developing into deep love. Sometimes this love is mutual; sometimes one person feels it much more strongly than the other. But because either or both of them are already married, and *eros* is forbidden, a conflict is created. They become ashamed of their love. Even though no impropriety has entered into their conduct, they become stricken with guilt at what they feel to be inordinate affection, so they strive to eradicate it.

But it should be remembered that while *eros* is forbidden to all except a married couple, *storge* and even *philia* are forbidden to none. Where *eros* is unlawful, then *philia* becomes the proper expression of love - whether between friends of the same sex or of the opposite sex. A Christian man may deeply love any woman with *philia*, and any Christian woman may so love a man. Love is not a thing of which to be ashamed. Only when love becomes lust (that is, unlawful *eros*) does it become a disgraceful thing. That is what the old version called "inordinate affection" (Col 3:5; and cp. Ez 23:11; Ro 1:26; 1 Th 4:5) - affection unfettered, desire undisciplined, love run wild.

But between any two people, the right kind of love, expressed in the right way, is always a beautiful thing, and it should be received as a gift of God.

Here, as in all these matters, the rule is still *epieikeia*. In your relationships with your neighbour, especially those you love, the pathway of graceful and reasonable good sense is to discover what expression of love is proper with each person, and then to pour all of your loving through that channel, and no other.

### D) *AGAPE* - Ethical Love

*Agape* (pronounced "a-gah-pay") is by far the most common word used in the NT to describe love as a Christian grace. It occurs as a noun almost 120 times, and as a verb (*agapao*) more than 130 times.

The surprising thing about agape is that it was not very popular with the classical Greek writers. In fact, they used it so rarely that it was once thought to have been a word invented by the early church to describe the new kind of love God has created for man through Christ. However, it is now known that *agape* was an ordinary Greek word, and a handful of occurrences have been found in ancient writings. But it remained an undistinguished word until the early Christians took hold of it, and ennobled it by using it to express that marvellous love which is uniquely a Christian grace.

It is worth asking why the Christians gave lesser emphasis to the other Greek words for love and concentrated on *agape?*

*William Barclay writes -*

> "It is true to say that all the other words had acquired certain flavours which made them unsuitable. 'Eros' had quite definite associations with the lower side of love; it had much more to do

with passion than with love. 'Storge' was very definitely tied up with family affection; it never had in it the width that the conception of Christian love demands.

"'Philia' was a lovely word, but it was definitely a word of warmth and closeness and affection; it could only properly be used of the near and the dear, and Christianity needed a much more inclusive word than that. Christian thought fastened on this word 'agape' because it was the only word capable of being filled with the content which was required.

"The great reason why Christian thought fastened on 'agape' is that 'agape' demands the exercise of the whole man. Christian love must not only extend to our nearest and our dearest, our kith and kin, our friends and those who love us; Christian love must extend to the Christian fellowship, to the neighbour, to the enemy, to all the world.

"Now, all the ordinary words for love are words which express an emotion. They are words which have to do with the heart. They express an experience which comes to us unsought, and, in a way, inevitably. We cannot help loving our kith and kin; blood is thicker than water. We speak about falling in love. That kind of love is not an achievement; it is something which happens to us and which we cannot help. There is no particular virtue in falling in love. It is something with which we have little or nothing consciously to do; it simply happens. But *agape* is far more than that."[10]

---

[10]   **New Testament Words,** pg. 20,21. SCM Press, London, 1971.

It can be seen then that there are three important differences between *agape* and the other kinds of love –

    i. ***Eros, storge,*** and ***philia*** are characterised as being more or less involuntary. They simply happen. They are based on some natural or instinctive affinity. They are selective. We easily love some people and not others. Hence no special virtue is attached to them, and no reward springs out of them save what is inherent in the joy of loving and being loved.

    ii. For that reason ***eros, storge,*** and ***philia*** cannot be commanded. Because they deal with instincts and emotions that are largely unbidden, we cannot be told to feel *eros, storge,* or *philia* for <u>anybody</u>, let alone <u>everybody</u>. Inherent in these three loves is a "liking" for the person loved. But we cannot be commanded to "like" all men, for there are many who are repulsive to us. Not even Christ "liked" all men. There were many for whom he had no affection at all - on the contrary, they filled him with loathing (cp. Mt 23:13-33; Lu 13:31-32).

    iii. But *agape* can be commanded; for it arises, not out of an unbidden emotion in the heart, but out of an act of the will. It is a triumph of the will over mere emotion.

William Barclay continues -

> "***Agape*** has to do with the **mind**: it is not simply an emotion which rises unbidden in our hearts; it is a principle by which we deliberately live. ***Agape*** has supremely to do with the will. It is a conquest, a victory, an achievement. No one ever naturally loved his enemies. To love one's enemies is a conquest of all our natural inclinations and emotions.
>
> "This *agape*, this Christian love, is not merely an emotional experience which comes to us unbidden and unsought; it is a deliberate principle of the

mind, and a deliberate conquest and achievement of the will. It is in fact the power to love the unlovable, to love people whom we do not like. Christianity does not ask us to love our enemies and to love men at large in the same way as we love our nearest and our dearest and those who are closest to us; that would be at one and the same time impossible and wrong. But it does demand that we should have at all times a certain attitude of the mind and a certain direction of the will towards all men, no matter who they are.

"What then is the meaning of this *agape*? The supreme passage for the interpretation of the meaning of agape is Mt 5:43-48. We are bidden to love our enemies. Why? In order that we should be like God. And what is the typical action of God that is cited? God sends his rain on the just and the unjust and on the evil and the good. That is to say - no matter what a man is like, God seeks nothing but his highest good.

"Let a man be a saint or let a man be a sinner. God's only desire is for that man's highest good. Now, that is what *agape* is. *Agape* is the spirit which says: 'No matter what any man does to me, I will never seek to do harm to him; I will never set out for revenge; I will always seek nothing but his highest good.' That is to say, Christian love, *'agape'*, **is unconquerable benevolence, invincible good will.**"[11]

Arising from this, three things may be said about ***agape*** -

---

[11]   Ibid. pg. 21,22

Christian love will not willingly release a friend (or even an enemy) to do evil, for to achieve that person's highest good may require an imposition of stern discipline. But Christian love will prevent any desire for revenge, and discipline will always be free of vindictiveness or spite.

Christian love is a product of the ministry of the Holy Spirit in the believer's life, for it is his task to "pour the love of God into our hearts" (Ro 5:5). How could anyone, apart from union with Christ, love an enemy? By definition, an enemy is someone you don't love! As William Barclay said, the biblical command to love your enemies is antagonistic to every natural instinct. How can you love those who hate you, who ill use you, who speak viciously against you? You can't! Not by yourself! But the Holy Spirit fills us with the love of God through Christ, and in this divine grace we can readily love all men, whether friend or foe, good or evil. We are commanded to yield ourselves to this love, and to resolve, not merely to refrain from doing harm to any person, but actively and positively to seek to do good to every person.

Christian love is based on God's love for us and our love for God: "We love him because he first loved us" (Jn 4:19). But we prove that we know the love of God by our love for the people of God. Does not Christ dwell in each believer? Is not every Christian made in the image of God? To say then that you love God is mockery, unless you also love those who bear his likeness, who like you are united with Christ, and who are members of the Father's family. The command is emphatic: "Love the brotherhood. Fear God." (1 Pe 2:17). It is interesting to notice that Peter places love of the brotherhood before fear of God. It is as though one were shown by the other. But in any case, we are obliged to offer all the saints of God an unfailing benevolence, goodwill, and kindness, which is encompassed by *agape*.

Hence we read -

> *"By this it may be seen who are the children of*
> *God, and who are the children of the devil: whoever*

*does not do right is not of God, <u>nor he who does not</u>*
*<u>love his brother (1 Jn 3:10)</u>*

*"We know that we have passed out of death into life*
*because we love the brethren.   <u>He who does not</u>*
*<u>love remains in death" (vs.14).</u>*

But notice that this love is not passive.  It is not just refraining from offering hurt to anyone.  Nor is it merely a feeling of goodwill.  ***Agape* seeks to do good; it reaches out in fellowship; it desires association; it cares; it wants to become involved; it cannot be merely neutral; it acts:** "Little children, let us not love in word or speech, but in deed and in truth" (vs.18).

Christian love is a reflection of the character of God
himself: "He who loves is born of God and knows
God.  He who does not love does not know God; for
God is love" (4:7-8).

It is important to remember that in all of these passages the word for "love" is *agape*, and that this ***agape*** is a Christian grace which cannot be experienced apart from Christ.  Hence John can say quite decisively that anyone who has ***agape*** must be born of God - for without the new birth one can have no experience of ***agape*.**  That person may know about ***agape*,** but cannot possibly possess it nor live it.

So John is able to add: "No one has ever seen God.  How then can we be sure God exists?  How can we be sure that we know him?  By this: if we love one another, we know that God abides in us, and his love is perfected in us" (vs. 12, paraphrased).

All of which leads to the rule: "**This commandment we have from him, <u>that he who loves God should love his brother also</u>**" (vs. 21). But remember: the love he is talking about is *agape*, and *agape* has nothing to do with emotion, but everything to do with will. You do not feel *agape*; but you will to do it. It is an attitude and an action, which has nothing to do with whether or not you like the person concerned. You may be empty of affection toward your neighbour, but you must be full of *agape* toward him.

To sum up: for your spouse you should be generous in **eros**; for your family, including the family of God in the church, you should have warm **storge**; for special friends God has given you **philia**; but to everyone - especially the brotherhood - the Lord commands you to express his own divine benevolence, which is **agape**.

# CHAPTER FOUR

# LOVING YOURSELF

Do not forget that underlying this entire series of Chapters on "Christian Life" is that remarkable principle expressed by Paul in Ph 4:5, "Let all men see your **moderation**." The Greek noun, you will recall, is *epieikeia* - that lovely grace of unselfish magnanimity.[12]

This Chapter applies the idea of *epieikeia* to your relationship with yourself.

Loving yourself too much, or loathing yourself too much, both violate the gentle rule of *epieikeia*. The more sensible advice of Paul is for you to have "a sober opinion" of yourself - neither thinking of yourself too highly nor too basely (Ro 12:3).

You are not better than you are; you are not worse than you are; at this moment you are simply what you are; and what you are is on the whole God's gift to you.

The first Chapters of this series have already guided you some distance along the path of Christian self-acceptance. The following paragraphs will take you a few steps further.

---

[12] For a fuller definition, see again page one of our first lesson and pages one and two of your third lesson.

## 1. <u>Some Important Principles</u>

### A) <u>Accept Yourself</u>

You must learn to accept yourself as you are today, and rejoice in it. Whatever you may become tomorrow, however you may improve, you cannot do so today. Today you are what God has made you, or what he has permitted you to become, and you should accept yourself with satisfaction. If you are not glad about who you are today, then you will probably be no happier tomorrow, for you will never be all that you may wish to be.

Now when I say that you should accept yourself with gladness, I mean accept your **weaknesses** as well as your **strengths**, for they both spring from the creative hand of God. The fact is, you are a package deal. No significant part of your personality or character, whether desirable or undesirable, can be removed without changing you into another person altogether. If God had wanted you to be that other person, he would have made you so in the first place. He is hardly going to do it at this stage of your life!

As "a package deal" your weaknesses and strengths are inseparable; they spring out of each other; they are inextricably inter-related; you cannot destroy one without destroying yourself. Do you really wish to commit suicide?

Many people are happy to retain their strengths and their virtues but how they lament their weaknesses! How earnestly they yearn to become another person! How bitterly they complain to God! But should the moulded clay say to its moulder, "Why have you made me thus?" (Ro 9:20). Surely the potter has full rights over the clay, "to make out of the same lump one vessel for beauty and another for menial use!" (vs. 21). So God has made you as it pleased him to make you. You cannot change your shape. So you may as well be content!

Now, I must admit that I am going to find it difficult to say without ambiguity what I want to say. My desire is to draw a picture of a Christian, living comfortably with himself and his Lord, at rest in his conscience, content to be the person God has made him, yet by no means static, nor passive. He has learned how to accept himself, but he does so only within dynamic growth and change. He recognises weakness without capitulating to it. He has found ways to prevent sin from making profit out of his weakness; he has learned how to turn his weakness to good advantage in the service of God. As I write, I am hoping that the Lord will help me to present that portrait in a way that neither minimises sin nor sets an impossible ideal.

In the previous paragraph I have used the word "weakness". That is not a very satisfactory choice, because it has in it a suggestion of sin, but I cannot find a better. As you read, try to remember that by "weakness" I do not mean sin (although any "weakness", of course, if it is indulged may lead to sin). Rather, I am using "weakness" to cover a broad spectrum of human infirmity, including such things as

     i. those aspects of your character which make you susceptible to certain kinds of sin, such as sensuality, selfishness, maliciousness, violence, and the like; and various personality traits; both those that are

     ii. negative: such as a disposition to indifference, callousness, aloofness, insularity, introspection, inferiority, timidity, legality, and the like; and

     iii. positive, but taken to excess: such as sympathy become sentimentality, extroversion become brashness, independence become arrogance, love become indulgence, pride become conceit, tolerance become licence, and the like.

We all find in ourselves some of these weaknesses. They are virtues gone astray; noble characteristics that in us are warped;

desirable traits that have become distorted; good things that in us have turned bad. Most sin, in fact, consists of some good thing taken to excess - as gluttony is an excess of eating, and immorality an excess of sensuality, and so on. Yet these "weaknesses" are all part of the total person God has made you, and generally speaking they cannot be eradicated without damaging the person God wants you to be. But they can be creatively accepted, controlled, and even transformed into attributes useful in the service of God.

One of the basic reasons why these "weaknesses" cannot be eradicated lies in the fact that they are often the reverse side of an admirable strength; for example, a loving disposition may have its reverse in reluctance to impose discipline; a passion for justice may have its reverse in a lack of mercy; a hunger for learning may have its reverse in stultifying sophistry, or perhaps indifference to human need; a skill in mechanics may have its reverse in a scorn of learning; and so on.

In God's world, every day has its night, and every positive has its negative; for every coin there are two sides, for every hill there is a valley, for every action there is a reaction; and for every strength there is a weakness, and for every weakness there is a strength. If you want to retain your strengths, then you will probably have to accept your weaknesses, for they belong to each other, and are as dependent upon each other as a tree and its roots. A strength is often the obverse of a weakness; a weakness is often the converse of a strength. But in any case, we are fashioned in such complexity, with such a mysterious amalgam of mind and emotion, body and soul, that the removal of any one part may disrupt the whole (Ps 139:1-6, 13-16). Unless you want your personal identity to be shattered, you will probably have to remain essentially the person you already are!

For most people, their problem lies neither in the existence of a weakness nor of a strength, but in the way they handle these things. They are guilty either of exaggerating the virtue, or of allowing unbridled expression to the vice. The next point, then, is very important ....

## B) <u>Handle Yourself Creatively</u>

Since you cannot change your basic personality, nor your inner identity, and since any attempt to do so is an insult to the God who fashioned you, your task is to discover what you are and then to handle yourself wisely and well.

So you must begin with that "sober opinion" I have mentioned above. You will be happy indeed if you can say with Don Quixote, "I know who I am!" Likewise, the Delphic oracle in ancient Greece never offered any wisdom higher than the saying graven on its temple wall: "KNOW THYSELF!"[13]

The task of knowing yourself, so that you neither think yourself better nor worse than you are, is not easy; a lifetime is scarcely long enough for such a discovery. But by merely being honest with yourself you will traverse a good part of the way. Delude yourself no longer. Acknowledge your strengths without pride; face your weaknesses without fear. You are strong in some ways, and weak in others. Admit to both, freely and without embarrassment; and then seek to handle both creatively. That involves two things -

i. You should praise God for your strengths, and set yourself to use them humbly and graciously for his glory. Away with that false piety, that spurious humility, which says that you have nothing, are nothing, and can do nothing for God! You are somebody, you do have something, and you can use your gift in the service of God. Paul was bold about it:

---

[13] Another famous moral precept carved upon the wall of the Delphic temple was **"Nothing too much"** – a kind of pagan parallel to the rule which underlies the entire series of lessons: epiekeia, that gracious Christian attribute of moderations

*"having gifts that differ according to the grace given to us, let us use them" (Ro 12:6).*

ii.  Certainly, you should serve God humbly, not arrogantly, and in dependence upon the grace that he himself supplies; but nevertheless you should serve him, employing every strength he has given you to produce fruit for his praise and for your own happiness. True Christian piety is wonderfully active, not supinely passive.

iii.  You should praise God for your weaknesses, for they provide you with an opportunity to acknowledge your need for his mercy, and to call upon his grace so that when you are weak you will be strong (2 Co 12:10; and cp. 13:9). You should remember also not to tempt God. In other words, do not place avoidable pressure on your weaknesses. As much as possible seek to escape influences that wrongfully inflame your hungers and drag you into failure.  Do not needlessly expose yourself to attack at the places where your defences are easily breached.  Let caution guard the soft places in your life.

Nor should you allow yourself to be enticed to accept a challenge or a task for which you are ill-equipped.  It is one thing to attempt the impossible for God; it is something else to attempt the improbable.  A wise man knows the difference (cp.  Mt 4:3-10).

Remember also, that your weakness may not be mine, as I hope to remember that my weakness may not be yours!  Which is only to say that godly prudence may forbid things to you that are quite permissible for me, and vice versa.  We must both answer to God, not to each other.

So there is a book I may read that you may not; there is an entertainment you may enjoy that for me is perilous; there is a task I may attempt that for you is folly; there is a place you may go that for me is the gate of hell; there is a friend I may have, or a relationship I may enjoy, that for you is an invitation to ruin.

Beware! Know yourself! Especially ....

## C) <u>Beware Of Your Strengths!</u>

I have often noticed that a person's strong points may be more a source of failure than his weak points. Speaking personally, I tend to be rather more apprehensive about the perils inherent in my strengths than I am about the dangers posed by my weaknesses.

I am painfully aware of my weaknesses. There is nothing subtle about them. When they snare me, it is like tripping over a stump. So I am on guard against them. I have learned how to combat their threat and to overcome it through Christ.

But the snare of strength is more cunning. Lulled into a false sense of security we become self-confident, careless, a little proud. Then the proverb is sadly fulfilled: "Pride goes before destruction, and a haughty spirit before a fall" (Pr 16:18). Paul gave a similar admonition: "Let any one who thinks that he stands take heed lest he fall" (1 Co 10:12).

The fact is, it is as difficult to handle your virtues as it is your vices. In both temptations we need the wisdom and grace of God in Christ. Discovery of that wisdom and grace will prevent your strengths from arrogantly causing you to advance ahead of the will of God, and also prevent your weaknesses from fearfully causing you to retreat away from the will of God. God knows you. He will not ask you to do more than your weaknesses permit, nor less than your strengths allow. It is enough for each of us simply to keep pace with God's purpose.

## D) <u>Mastering Your Weaknesses</u>

You do by now understand, I hope, that when I talk about "weaknesses", I do not mean sin, even though sin may arise out of the weakness. We can never live comfortably with sin, not even for a moment. I may (in fact, must) become reconciled to the "weaknesses" that are an inherent and necessary part of the total person God has made me; but I can never accept even the slightest sin. All sin is hated by those who love God. My "weakness" can be made my friend; but sin can never be other than a wretched and despicable enemy, a foe to be relentlessly pursued and destroyed by the power of the cross.

However, sin commonly takes advantage of my weakness to entice me to evil, hence the weakness itself becomes identified in my mind with sin. But the two must be kept separate.

Paul uses an interesting word in one place, the Greek word "*akrasia*". It occurs in 1 Co 7:5, in a discourse about the duties of a married couple to each other: "Do not refuse one another except perhaps by agreement for a season, that you may devote yourselves to prayer; but then come together again, lest Satan tempt you through lack of self-control."

The words in italics translate *akrasia*, which the lexicons define as: *want of power, lack of strength, not master of one's self, intemperate, unruly appetite, incontinent.* Putting these ideas together we may say that "*akrasia*" identifies those particular places where we happen to be weak, where we lack full personal mastery. There is an unruliness in these areas, a want of control, an urge to intemperance. We might call them "points of incontinence."

Scripture and life both indicate that we all have these points of incontinence. They are the flabby underbelly of your soul. There Satan aims his fiery darts.

Here then is the place of temptation. Here the attack is mounted - for what army would ever besiege a castle at the place where its walls are impregnable? The enemy of your soul shrewdly seeks the gap in your defences and bears down upon you there.

If these things are so, then it is wisdom to know your own points of incontinence and to take special steps to defend them. Here are some suggestions -

i. You have no choice but to accept your weakness for the moment, and to learn to live with it comfortably. The topography of your life and character, the way the great Architect has put your castle together, may prevent you from effectively rebuilding that weak part of the wall to make it as impregnable as the rest of your defences.

ii. But though you may accept the weakness, you should never capitulate to it, nor to the enemy who seeks to take advantage of it. Acknowledging that you are susceptible to failure in some areas in your life is not the same as surrendering to that defeat. We are called to conquer! We should recognise points of incontinency only so that we may take prudent steps either to eradicate them, to transform them, or to guard them more stringently, so that no defeat is possible.

Thus many a mediaeval fortress had to accept a fault in the lay of the land that created a weak spot in the castle's defences. But the prudent owners neither abandoned the fortress nor easily surrendered to the enemy, but rather took special pains to mount heavy defences at those points where the castle was most vulnerable.

Some points of incontinence, by patient perseverance, by faith, or by growth in maturity, can be removed altogether (as the ancient barons might have dug a moat or levelled a small hill, to make their domain safer). But other such points, which are an integral part of your particular personality, must be wrought upon and adapted until they become part of the beautiful whole person God desires you to be. For example, a disposition to

- timidity may become sensitive concern for the weak.
- sensuality may become imaginative passion for righteousness.
- reclusiveness may become vigilance in prayer.
- arrogance may become boldness against the kingdom of darkness.
- aloofness may become objectivity in counsel.

In other words, seek to eradicate only what is actually sinful or antagonistic to God's purpose for your life. Otherwise be content to be the person you are, and then find ways to use what you are for the glory of God.

What sin may have warped in you, by patient growth, by believing appropriation of the promises of God, may then be transformed back into useful tools for divine service.

## E) Set A High Standard

Every Christian should set a high standard. You should develop a noble self-image, an exciting and admirable vision of the kind of person you want to be, and a clear concept of the person God has called you to be in Christ. Life should then be geared to attaining that goal.

But wisdom is needed. It is foolish to create a standard so high that it is actually unattainable. To do that is to invite frequent failure, which leads to a self-image of defeat. If you experience continual failure in one area of your life, it will gradually spill over into every part of your life. The walls of a fortress need to be breached in only one place for the whole castle to fall. An image of yourself endlessly defeated in one thing will irresistibly erode the victorious image you may have of yourself in other things.

Some people, however, do seek to escape the guilt of failure by unconsciously setting themselves an impossible goal, so they cannot then be blamed for failing to attain it - "After all," they reason, "no one else could have done it either!" Thus they quieten the accusing voice of conscience. But the Spirit of God is not deceived so easily - see Lu 14:28-30.

You should certainly dream up a picture of your life as a noble "tower", a splendid castle - but let it be one that you can realistically build with God's help. Set yourself a goal that will stretch your resources and engage your faith, but avoid setting it so far beyond reach that you will inevitably perish in the hiatus between faith and presumption.

## F) Love Yourself

God loves you! Why should you not love yourself. Only a peculiar piety imagines that God is pleased with an attitude of endless self-denigration. He looks at you and generally likes what he sees. You should look in the mirror and like what **you** see! That would cease to be true only if you are fallen away from his grace and have given yourself to the life of a reprobate. But if you are walking with the Lord as nearly as you can, sincerely desiring to do his will and to conform to the image he has of you in Christ, then you can and should be pleased with the person he has made you to be.

If you are God's child in Christ, then the Father loves you. He may need to train and discipline you (He 12:5-11), but his love remains the same. Just as you are commanded to "love the brotherhood" because each Christian is made in God's image, indwelt by Christ, and belonging to the one eternal family, so must you love yourself for the same reasons.

If you cannot live lovingly and harmoniously with yourself you will probably find just as much distress and difficulty in your relationships with other people. If you don't like yourself you will probably have trouble liking anyone.

It is wisdom to place only a little emphasis on your faults and much emphasis on your virtues - although a certain kind of popular piety finds masochistic satisfaction in doing the opposite. Virtues are scorned as having no merit, while sins are magnified as though they were the only deeds actually done by the Christian. To such people, no commendation is due for even the noblest of deeds; but each sin, even the least of them, is spotlighted for awful condemnation.

That is folly.

You would do well to apply to yourself the advice that Matthew Prior - that witty inventor of epigrams - gave some 300 years ago to husbands:

> *Be to her virtues very kind,*
> *Be to her faults a little blind*[14]

So should be your attitude toward yourself. I do not mean that you should condone sin, nor belittle its guilt, but that there should be a balance, an *epieikeia*, **about your handling of both your virtues and your faults.**

The Bible tells you what to do about your faults - Ja 5:16-17; 1 Jn 1:6-9. Once you have done that, forget them; then set about praising God for all the nice things that are true about you. To stay wallowing in self-pity, confessing defeat, always deprecating yourself, insulting God by inferring that he has made you poorly, hardly reflects a godly frame of mind.

What is even more tragic is to find so many people who believe that God himself wants them to endlessly berate and demean themselves. What a sad delusion! Surely your Father desires you to stand tall in Christ, conscious of the beauty he has wrought in you through the new birth, utilising the grace he has poured into you by the Holy Spirit, and reflecting the radiance of the new creation you have now become! (See 2 Co 5:16-18; 4:5-7; Ep 1:3-8; 2:16-20; Col. 3:1-3; etc).

---

[14] From the Poem, "**An English Padlock**" written in 1707. The stanza has two other lines that were no doubt popular in more chauvenistic times, but happily are forgotten in these sweetly enlightened days –

Let all her ways be unconfined,
and clap your padlock – on her mind!

# CONCLUSION

The purpose of this first Section has been to try to show you how to adopt a balanced and mature attitude in the way you love the world, and your neighbour and yourself. I have endeavoured to avoid extremes, and also to avoid rules or concepts that are useful for some people and not for others. The scriptures are universal in their truth, and any teaching based on scripture should be equally universal.

Perhaps nothing has been written above that you did not already know, but it is always good to be reminded of what you know (2 Pe 1:12-15). Yet there are many fine Christians who could find a wonderful release and a new pleasure in life through embracing the principles presented here.

(The next Section will explore the Christian's place in society.)

# SECTION TWO

# LOVING YOUR NEIGHBOURS

# INTRODUCTION

*"Do not get drunk with wine, for that is debauchery; but be filled with the Spirit, addressing each other in psalms and hymns and spiritual songs, singing and making melody to the Lord with all your heart, always and for everything giving thanks in the name of our Lord Jesus Christ to God the Father. Be subject to each other out of reverence for Christ" (Ep 5:18-21).*

Notice the sequence of five present participles -

    addressing
    singing
    making
    giving
    subjecting

The first four are commonly and cheerfully linked with the ministry of the Spirit, but by a kind of unconscious consensus the fifth is almost universally ignored. There are many people who desire to be filled with the Spirit so that they may preach, sing, make melody, and praise; but how few there are who seek the fullness of the Spirit so that they may submit!

Yet Paul did not dare to say that by the fullness of the Holy Spirit we may address each other without adding that by the same Spirit we must be subject to each other. Rather, he is careful to stress that the enthusiasm, life, and song that Holy Spirit baptism generates should not be expressed by each person doing his own thing, but rather through genuine fellowship and through humble submission of each to the other.

The end result of being filled with the Spirit, and of our singing, thanksgiving, ministry, and fellowship, should be, not arrogant independence, not solitary conceit, but submission.

Here then is a revelation: the way to cause divine life to flow in the church is for all of its members, by the power of the Holy Spirit, to be subject to each other, in sincere recognition of each other's dignity in Christ. But if the members of the church are unwilling to submit to each other in love, or to yield to the disciplinary authority of the church, then they must accept the penalty of such immaturity.

The price of complete independence is stunted development. What father can form his children into mature, well-balanced adults, if they run away from home whenever he seeks to discipline them? His fear of losing them will prevent him from properly correcting them. The aphorism of Juan Ortiz is true: "There is no formation without submission." As clay must submit to the potter, as marble to the sculptor, as a child to its parents, so must each Christian submit to the brotherhood. Without this submission mature development becomes impossible.

This idea of submission is expressed some thirty times in the NT, and even more often in the OT. It is an important part of Christian doctrine. It is also widely misunderstood. Extremes are apparent here as elsewhere - there are those who resist all authority; and there are those who allow too much authority. We seek rather the godly path of "*epieikeia*".

# CHAPTER FIVE

# SUBMISSION IN THE FAMILY

The first place we all encounter authority is in the home. There we learn dependence and discipline - and this is true even in the most unstructured homes. No group of people can survive together without some measure of mutual restraint, or some yielding of personal desires to the needs of the larger group.

Christian families, of course, will seek to be structured according to the biblical pattern. It is my intention to examine that structure in just one area: authority and submission. If those matters are rightly understood, then most of the others will fall easily into place.

## THE SUBMISSION OF CHILDREN TO THEIR PARENTS

### The Nature Of This Submission

*"Children, obey your parents in the Lord, for this is right" (Ep 6:1)*

To establish this rule, Paul appeals to two things –

### 1. The Propriety Of The Rule

The motive for obedience is not exclusively gratitude nor love, important though those two emotions may be, but rather -

## A)  Reverence for Christ

Children are to obey their parents "in the Lord", which means, because of the love, respect, and honour they hold for Christ, whom they acknowledge as Lord and Saviour.  In this they have the good example of Christ himself: "He went down with (his parents) and came to Nazareth, and was **obedient** to them" (Lu 2:51).

Obedience shown by children to their parents is an indication that they belong to the kingdom of God, and not the kingdom of darkness.  As Albert Barnes writes:

> "The government of God is what a perfect family government would be; and to accustom a child to be obedient to a parent is designed to be one method of leading him to be obedient to God.  No child that is disobedient to a father and mother will be most likely to become a Christian and an heir of heaven."[15]

## B)  The fitness of obedience

Children are to obey their parents, simply because "this is right." There is a certain fitness, a propriety, about an obedient child which is utterly lacking from a child who is rebellious and wayward.  This fitness is established by –

i.   Natural law

The consensus of every generation, in every land, from the beginning of recorded history until now, has been that children ought to be submissive and obedient to their parents.  A society falls into desperate straits when children become its oppressors (Is 3:12), and perilous times have arrived when the young are "proud,

---

[15]   **Notes On The New Testament**; Kregel Publications, Grand Rapids, Michigan; 1966; pg. 1008

arrogant, abusive, disobedient to their parents, ungrateful, unholy" (2 Ti 3:2).

Nature itself teaches that the young ought to obey those upon whom they depend for sustenance, training, and protection. Natural motives of gratitude, affection, and appreciation, ought to teach the young to honour and respect their elders. A humble sense of their own immaturity and inexperience ought to cause the young to adhere to the guidance and wisdom of the adults among whom they dwell.

To require obedience from children, then, is not to act against natural law, but rather to conform to it.

### ii. Divine law

Children should obey their parents primarily because God commands that they should do so. Paul simply asserts that obedience is "right". It is right because God has said that it is right. No further reason is really necessary, nor can any proper argument be raised against it. And the place where God has said it is in the sacred scriptures -

> *The Fifth Commandment: "Honour your father and your mother" (Ex 20:12).*
>
> *"Whoever strikes his father or his mother shall be put to death ... whoever curses his father or his mother shall be put to death" (21:15,17). The extreme penalty may no longer be applicable; but this law nonetheless exposes the profound anger God feels against those who dishonour their parents (cp. also De 21:18-21; 27:16).*
>
> *"Hear, my son, your father's instruction, and reject not your mother's teaching; for they are a fair*

*garland for your head, and pendants for your neck"*
*(Pr 1:8,9).*

*"If one curses his father or his mother, his lamp
will be put out in utter darkness" (20:20)*

*"The eye that mocks a father and scorns to obey a
mother will be picked out by the ravens of the valley
and eaten by the vultures" (30:17).*

*Jesus said: "God commanded, 'Honour your father
and your mother;' and, 'He who speaks evil of
father or mother, let him surely die.'" (Mt 15:4).*

♦ and there are many other similar references.

Obedience offered to a parent is reckoned as obedience to God;
while disobedience to a parent is reckoned as rebellion against
God. A child who desires to please God can do so primarily by
submitting gladly to his mother and father.

## 2. The Promise Of The Rule

If it is right that children should obey their parents, it is also
rewarding. Paul reminds us that alongside this commandment of
first importance, a promise is placed: "that it may be well with you,
and that you may live long on the earth" (cp. Ex 20:12; De 5:16).
It cannot be claimed that this promise is literally fulfilled in every
obedient child, for there are some godly children who are
overtaken by misfortune, and some ungodly children who live long
and prosperously.[16]

---

[16] That is they may appear to do so; but at a deeper level it could be said that
they can have no inner peace, nor any real contentment – for no-one can live
with true happiness whose only goal is graveyard putrefaction.

However, while the promise may not be fully outworked in the life of every godly child, it is certainly true to say –

      i.   that even if the promise of "long" life is not always fulfilled, the promise of eternal life most certainly is! Likewise, the promise "it shall be well with you" is always fulfilled - at least in its deepest sense of spiritual wellbeing.

      ii.   that it is generally true to say that obedient children do tend to grow into mature, responsible, and prosperous adults, whereas rebellious children are prone to erratic and irresponsible development, and to personal failure. It is also true to say that a society built around stable and disciplined homes is an enduring society, and the enemies of that people will not easily prevail against them; whereas the collapse of a nation's homes has usually presaged the ruin of that nation. History is replete with examples of this principle.

## The Modifiers Of This Submission

The demand for submission is not unqualified.

There is a point beyond which parents may not insist on obedience. On the contrary, at that point parents must themselves submit to the rights and personalities of their children.

Children are neither toys nor chattels. They are made in God's image more than they are made in the image of their parents; they bear a divine likeness that is far more compelling than any human likeness. The ultimate task of any parent is not to rear a child to conform to the father's will, but to the Father's will. The parents' most important role is to help their children discover the purpose of God, and then to guide them into realising that purpose.

So parents should seek to bring out in their children the image of God, not their own images. Parents fail when they stifle in their children anything that is part of the unique gift of God to each child. Parents succeed when they enable their children to discover all that they are and possess, and when they help them to develop fully their own particular talents, abilities, and personalities.

An important principle becomes apparent here, namely, that authority always carries with it a commensurate responsibility.

Any attempt to abrogate or ignore this responsibility is to step from authority into autocracy. Those who wish to rule must also serve, and only those who honour this obligation to serve may properly assume the right to rule.

Further, those from whom obedience is required (child, wife, servant, employee, citizen) may rightly protest against any abuse of authority that arises from a refusal to submit to the obligations authority entails. In the economy of God neither authority, nor obedience to authority, is ever absolute, unqualified, or irresponsible. Those who rule should seek to do so with moderation *(epieikeia)*, not as dictators. Those who serve should not lapse into servility, but retain their freedom of spirit, and above all their freedom to do the will of God - and this they can do even when overwhelmed by the greater strength of a tyrant.

There are times when it may be more godly to resist tyranny and injustice than to yield passively to it - but beware lest resistance itself becomes ungodly and incurs the anger of God. Resistance that leads to anarchy cannot be condoned, for the wellbeing of the church, and the successful propagation of the gospel, both substantially depend upon domestic and civic tranquillity.

Now we are to examine how this principle of tempered and responsible authority applies to the degree of submission that parents may require from their children -

## 1. Children Need Obey Only "In The Lord"

Barnes comments on the meaning of "in the Lord":

> "That is, as far as their commandments agree with those of God, and no farther. No parent can have a right to require a child to steal, or lie, or cheat, or assist him in committing murder, or in doing any other wrong thing. No parent has a right to forbid a child to pray, to read the Bible, to worship God, or to make a profession of religion ... In all cases, God is to be obeyed rather than man. When a parent, however, is opposed to a child; when he expresses an unwillingness that a child should attend a particular church, or make a profession of religion, such opposition should, in all cases, be a sufficient reason for the child to pause and re-examine the subject. He should pray much, and think much, and enquire much before, in any case, he acts contrary to the will of a father or mother; and when he does do it, he should state to them, with great gentleness and kindness, that he believes he ought to love and serve God."[17]

## 2. Parents Must Not "Provoke Their Children To Anger"

Bengel comments on this: "Despondency is the bane of youth." Which is to say that parental rule may become so harsh, or unjust, or indulgent, that the spirit of the child is broken, and he is then aroused into angry rebellion. Coddling or caning a child too much, will both cause him equal harm. William Hendriksen gives the following list of ways in which parents may foolishly stir their children to indignant revolt -[18]

---

[17]   Op. cit. Pg. 1008

[18]   See **New Testament Commentary**, "Ephesians", pg. 261, 262; Baker Book House, Grand Rapids, Michigan, 1972.

- by over-protection and shielding them from all risks, even those that are a necessary part of growth and achievement.

- by favouritism and partiality, preferring one child above another.

- by endless discouragement and petty criticism, never offering any praise, thus destroying the child's self-confidence and his creative urge.

- by failure to make allowance for the fact that the child is growing up, has a right to have ideas of his own, and need not be an exact copy of his father (or mother) to be a success.

- by neglect of the child's training, care, and upbringing.

- by bitter words, outright cruelty, and bouts of unrestrained anger.

Francis Foulkes adds: "It is right for parents to demand obedience, but there must not be 'capricious exercise of authority' (Robinson). Discipline is essential in the home; but not unnecessary rules and regulations, and endless petty correction by which children are 'discouraged' (Col 3:21).[19]

### 3. Parents Must "Nourish" Their Children

The RSV uses the rather tame translation, "bring them up." The Greek word means not merely to "rear" a child, but to nourish him, to rear him carefully. Hendriksen translates it, "rear them tenderly"; Calvin suggests, "let them be fondly cherished." The idea is one of a father (and mother) accepting responsibility under God for the welfare, training, and development of the child, recognising that he is God's steward of this young life. The child is not his, but God's.

---

[19] See **Tyndale NT Commentary,** "Ephesians", pg. 165. Tyndale Press, London. 1966

The Greek word for "bring them up" or "rear tenderly" is used only twice in the NT, both times by Paul, and both in Ephesians - 5:29; and 6:4 (our text). The first of those references may be translated: "No man ever hates his own flesh, but fondly nourishes and cherishes it." It cannot be without significance that Paul chose the same word to describe the parents' care of themselves and their care of their children. Just as a man lovingly and tenderly nourishes himself, looking on himself with sympathy and toleration, treating himself with pardon and grace, so must he cherish and care for his children. Failure to do this forfeits his right to demand obedience from them.

## 4. In The Discipline And Instruction Of The Lord"

If the previous restraints are heeded, then parental discipline will be neither too lax nor too harsh, nor will parents fail in their duty to supervise the education of their children.

It ought to be remembered that the Bible stresses that parents, not the church, nor the state, are primarily responsible for the training of children. Yet all too often in our society parents have surrendered their duty in this matter. It is common now for parents to allow the state to take full responsibility for the secular education of their children, and to demand that the church take full responsibility for their spiritual education.

But scripture will not allow that.

While parents may freely make use of, and co-operate with, church and state, God has given to them and to them alone the right and responsibility of ensuring that their children are tenderly reared in the "discipline" and "instruction" of the Lord. Let us look at these two aspects of child training -

## A) <u>The discipline of the Lord</u>

The idea of discipline is not so popular today as it was in other times, but it is no less necessary. According to Hendriksen, "instruction" refers to what is <u>said</u> to the child - it is training by means of the spoken word; but "discipline" refers to what is <u>done</u> to the child - it is training "by means of rules and regulations, rewards, and when necessary, punishments."

Here are some scripture references to discipline: Pr 13:24; 19:18; 22:6,15; 23:13, 14; 29:15, 17; He 12:5-11.

But it must be remembered that this discipline must be "of the Lord"; that is, it will not be administered with spite, nor merely to satisfy hurt pride, nor in unreasoning anger. It will be controlled discipline, matched in severity to the offence, reflecting the righteous law of God, tempered by compassion for the weaknesses of the child, and guided by a genuine desire to promote the child's growth in character and maturity.

Loving discipline will seek also to achieve its goals by proffering rewards rather than by threatening penalties. The rewards for good behaviour will at least match, if not surpass, the punishment for bad behaviour.

Scripture makes it abundantly plain that God deals with his own people in the same way: it speaks many times of the "chastening of the Lord"; but even more often of the marvellous benefits he heaps upon the righteous! You will find it profitable to check your concordance and to make a list of both sets of references.

Parents, then, are not given an unrestricted right to discipline their children. Capricious and arbitrary punishment is forbidden. Parental control must be exercised within the rules framed by scripture. Certain things follow –

i. Parents who fail to discipline their children properly, and those who discipline them too severely, are likely to induce rebellion and to lose the love and respect of their children.

ii. Parents who discipline their children wisely and who make it known to their children that this discipline is a reflection of the righteous law of God, may assume that their children will respond to it without resentment. Children who observe that their parents are obedient to God will accept the justice of that same obedience being required of them. A child will usually submit willingly to a parent who is sensitive to the needs of the child, and who acknowledges the rights the child has in God.

iii. Parents who discipline their children wisely may expect to retain the love and respect of their children; they may also assume that the discipline will achieve its desired effect, and that it will fix their children in the ways of righteousness. God-fearing parents nurture God-fearing children. This rule sometimes fails, it is not absolute; but there is a strong presumption that a child will not depart from the way in which he has been trained.

### B) The instruction of the Lord

"A wise son", we are told, "makes a glad father" (Pr 10:1). But a son will not attain to that wisdom unless he is instructed to do so; hence the parent has a duty to teach, and the child has a duty to heed. This also is a frequent theme in scripture: De 4:9, 10; 6:6-9; 11:19,20; 31:12,13; Ps 34:11; Pr 13:1; 15:5,20; 17:2,21,25; 19:13,26.

This instruction should appertain to every part of life, secular and sacred, academic and moral, social and cultural; but special emphasis is placed by scripture on the child's religious upbringing. Above all, children should be taught that wisdom begins with the fear of the Lord.

In reply to the objection that children should not be subject to indoctrination in religious matters, the following points may be raised- [20]

     i.  We instruct our children in many other things without being accused of destroying their independence and objectivity, so why should we not instruct them in religion?  To fail to do so is simply to leave their minds uncultivated in one of the most vital areas of thought and life.

     ii.  No man can avoid inculcating his religious attitudes on his children.  What atheist or unbeliever fails to convey to his children his ideas on religion, or makes any serious attempt to hide those ideas, or deliberately exposes his children to religious concepts?  Such men are usually as anxious to prevent their children from becoming religious as the Christian is to train his children in the ways of the Lord!

> "Men teach by example, by incidental remarks, by the neglect of that which they regard as of no value. A man who does not pray, is teaching his children not to pray; he who neglects the public worship of God, is teaching his children to neglect it; he who does not read the Bible, is teaching his children not to read it." (Barnes).

     iii.  *True religious teaching does not narrow the mind; it rather broadens it, and makes the mind better able to perceive all that is true in God's world.  Error and deceit are the things that limit a child's horizon and imprison him in darkness.*

     iv.  *"If a man does not teach his children truth, others will teach them error."*

---

[20]   They are drawn from Barnes, op.cit., pg. 1009

v. *For a Christian, no subject holds greater importance than true religion, and it is inconceivable that Christian parents should be asked to forsake their duty to train their children in the discipline and instruction of the Lord.*

The conclusion is then: in Christian families, children are to submit to the rule of their parents, and parents are to submit to the right of their children. This combined principle of authority and submission begins in the family, and then extends out (as we shall see) to the church and the state.

## THE SUBMISSION OF A WIFE TO HER HUSBAND

"Wives, be subject to your husbands, as to the Lord. For the husband is the head of the wife as Christ is the head of the church ... As the church is subject to Christ, so let wives be subject in everything to their husbands. Husbands, love your wives, as Christ loved the church and gave himself up for her ... Even so, husbands should love their wives as their own bodies. He who loves his wife loves himself" (see Ep 5:22-33).

The scriptures never deviate from the principle that in a godly home the wife will submit to the authority of her husband. See Ge 3:16; Es 1:20-22; 1 Co 11:1-16; 14:34; Ep 5:22-33; Col 3:18; 1 Ti 2:11,12; Tit 2:5; 1 Pe 3:1,6; and cp. also Pr 12:4; 14:1; 18:22; 19:13,14; 25:24; 30:21-23; 31:10-31.

But neither do the scriptures deviate from the principle that the husband owes specific duties to his wife: Ex 21:10; De 24:5; Pr 5:15-19; Ec 9:9; Mal 2:14-16; Ep 5:22-23; 1 Ti 5:8; 1 Pe 3:7.

Unqualified authority is not given to the husband, neither is unqualified obedience required of the wife.

There is here, as always, a merging of authority and submission, a requirement of *epieikeia*.

There are areas where husband and wife both have authority over each other, and areas where they must both submit to each other –

1.  There are many ways in which women are fully equal to men:

    ♦   they have an equal status in worship and prayer for God makes no distinction between man or woman (Ga 3:28; Ac 10:34).

    ♦   they are equal inheritors with men of the kingdom of God.

    ♦   they are demonstrably the intellectual equals of men, and equally as skilled in the arts, and equally as capable in many other areas of commerce and culture.

2.  There are clearly areas in which women must be acknowledged as superior to men: in loveliness, in grace, in tenderness, in sympathy, and in other uniquely feminine qualities. In these things they reflect their special place as the culminating glory of God's work of creation.

3.  Within the family, God has made man the head, and his authority should be gladly acknowledged. This authority is based on the principle of primogeniture - 1 Co 11:8-9; 1 Ti 2:13; and it is strengthened by the fact that Eve was deceived before Adam - Ge 3:16; 1 Ti 2:14. The scriptures make it abundantly plain that adherence to this divine pattern will bring prosperity to the family, while violation of it will bring fracture and misery - Ps 128:1-3; Pr 21:9,19; 2:24; 27:15-16.

4.  The chief argument for a husband's authority is found by Paul in a comparison of the family with the church. He says that husband and wife have a relationship of love and authority similar to that which exists between Christ and the church (Ep 5:22-33) -

*"The husband is the head of the wife as Christ is the head of the church" (vs. 23).*

*"As the church is subject to Christ, so let wives be subject in everything to their husbands" (vs.24).*

*"Wives, be subject to your husbands as to the Lord" (vs. 22).*

*"Let the wife see that she respects her husband" (vs.33).*

If the analogy presented by Paul is accepted, if it is true that a husband stands in the same relation to his wife as Christ does to the church, then the authority of the husband is unassailable. A Christian wife who resists her husband's authority without adequate reason to do so is in fact resisting Christ. If she isolates herself from her husband, if she disrupts the marriage relationship, then she may well place herself outside of the protection of Christ - for normally God's favour, protection, and provision will flow to the wife through her husband.

For this reason Paul infers that the husband is the "saviour" - the sustainer, guardian, provider, covering - of his wife, just as Christ is of the church (vs. 23).

Apparently Paul gained his authority for this analogy from the OT, which contains numerous references to Israel as the bride of God, and to God himself as Israel's husband - see Is 54:5-6; 62:4,5; Je 31:32; Ez 16:8-14; Ho 2:16; etc.

The terminology used in those passages leaves no doubt about the view of marriage held by ancient Israel: it was a covenant relationship which brought to the wife many benefits and much happiness; but it was nevertheless one in which she was subordinate to her husband, as Israel was to God.

It was also a relationship in which the husband covenanted to love his wife dearly and faithfully, and to provide for her, as God did to Israel. God said that he hated divorce, because it meant a violation of this sacred covenant, and it injured the concept of marriage as an essentially spiritual union which reflects the union of God with his own covenant people (Mal 2:13-16).

So the scriptures, in both testaments, establish the marriage contract as one which equally binds husband and wife: she to love and obey; he to love and comfort.

5.   This subordination of the wife to her husband is one of office only; in no way can it be said to imply inferiority of person or of status in the kingdom of God. The woman has a value in every way equal to that of the man.

But within the structure of her home, and for its salvation and wellbeing, she is required by God to yield authority to her husband. In this the woman has an example in Christ himself -

> *"I want you to understand that the head of every man is Christ, the head of a woman is her husband, and the head of Christ is God" (1 Co 11:3).*

I cannot improve on Albert Barnes' comment:

> "Christ, as Mediator, has consented to assume a subordinate rank, and to recognise God the Father as superior in office. Hence he was obedient in all things as a Son; he submitted to the arrangement required in redemption; he always recognised his subordinate rank as Mediator, and always regarded God as the Supreme Ruler, even in the matter of redemption. The sense is, that Christ, throughout his entire work, regarded himself as occupying a subordinate station to the Father; and that it was

> proper from his example to recognise the propriety
> of rank and station everywhere."[21]

The operative word is "consent". Subordination could not be forced upon Christ. In his person and in his attributes he stands equal with God (Ph 2:6; Col 1:15-19). But, in order to secure our redemption, he consented to adopt a subordinate role, and to place himself under the Father's authority.

So also, following Christ's example, the wife is called upon to voluntarily submit herself to her husband, to acknowledge him as head of the family, and by so doing to promote the honour and prosperity of her family under God.

And what is true of her, is also true of her husband, and of all the people of God. Just as Christ, to achieve our salvation, accepted the office of Mediator, and placed himself under the Father's authority, so should we all, in our own outworking of that salvation, be willing to accept the rank God has given us.

    6.  But what should a Christian wife do when her husband is an unbeliever?

    A)  See 1 Pe 3:1-4. Let the wife submit to her husband as far as she may do so without violating her conscience or the command-ments of God.

Peter suggests that by the sweet winsomeness of her faith, and the quiet beauty of her life she may win her husband to Christ. However, there is no guarantee of this (1 Co 7:16),[22] and she should continue to be submissive whether or not he becomes a Christian.

---

[21]  Ibid. pg. 753.

[22]  In the RSV (and other translations), 1 Co 7:16 reads: "Wife, how do you know whether you will save your husband? Husband, how do you know whether you will save your wife?"

B) This submission cannot be absolute. There is a point beyond which a wife is not required by God to submit, and a further point beyond which she dare not submit. Briefly, she is not required to submit to her husband if he is significantly failing to honour his side of the marriage contract; and she must not submit to him if he commands her to act contrary to the laws of God -

i. When a husband fails significantly to honour, love, and comfort his wife, the scriptures, by inference and by clear statement, release her from the duty of submission.

> *Ex 21:7-11; De 21:10-14. Even a slave-wife was legally free to leave her husband if he "diminished" her "food, clothing, or marital rights". The idea here is that, as his wife, she was entitled to live as pleasantly and richly as he did himself; he could not force her to be content with the more meagre fare given to the other household slaves. He was to treat her generously and lovingly. If he failed to do this, she could appeal to the court for release from her bond to him. A war captive was to be similarly treated.*

> *De 22:13-21. A woman who was unjustly accused by her husband could bring him to court and secure a heavy penalty against him.*

> *1 Co 7:4. Husbands and wives have the "rule" over each other's bodies. If either withholds marital rights from the other, without sufficient reason, or without the other's consent, then the offended party may act to terminate the marriage.*

> *1 Co 7:12-16. Where an unbelieving spouse is "content" to dwell with a believer, the marriage must be maintained; it continues to be a holy union in the sight of God. But "content" must mean more*

*than merely living under the same roof, or sleeping in the same bed. It surely implies that the unbeliever is not offended by the faith of the Christian spouse, nor is there any serious restraint on the Christian's freedom to attend worship and to serve God. In other words the "peace" of the marriage is not seriously disrupted (vs. 15). Both partners still love each other, or at least they are both still kindly and faithfully fulfilling their obligations to each other.*

The sanctity and beauty of marriage cannot be upheld by preserving a union which contains only bitterness, strife, and misery. Some commentators may differ from this interpretation of the passage, but this seems to me to be its spirit and its intention.

If that is so, then a Christian wife is bound to submit to her husband, and to maintain the marriage, only insofar as he is truly her *husband*, not merely by law, but by *behaviour*. That is, he is to her all that a good husband should be. I do not suppose that God requires a Christian woman to submit to a man who incessantly abuses her, whether verbally, physically, mentally, emotionally, or spiritually. I say this, however, assuming that the wife has not invited abuse by her own arrogance or foolishness. I am assuming that she has made every effort to conform to the letter and the spirit of 1 Pe 3:1-6, 8-12.

*1 Co 11:11-12. Paul, having strongly asserted that a wife must submit to her husband (vs. 3-10), hastens to add a qualifier. He is not satisfied to place such unrestrained power in the man's hand! So he insists that the man is as much indebted to the woman as the woman is to the man. Which is to say that as much as the husband may require submission from his wife, just so much may the wife require honour from her husband. Nor should the husband be permitted to prevail merely because of his superior strength. If he fails to give due honour to his wife (1 Pe 3:7), and his wife is unable because of weakness to protect herself, then church and society should come to her defence.*

Marriage is a partnership of two people who are equally indebted to God (1 Co 11:12), neither of whom have rights superior to those of the other, and both of whom have equal duties to each other. The church, in particular, ought to refrain from encouraging the idea that the husband has prerogatives greater than those of his wife. Rather, it ought to apply the same pressure on both partners to be true to their vows to each other. It is true that "the husband is the head of the wife" (vs.3, ff.); but this is matter of office only (as I have already said), and the responsibilities it entails more than outweigh any advantage it may confer.

The inference of these passages, and of others like them, is that no wife is bound to stay in a marriage situation that has become cruel and intolerable. She cannot be obliged to submit to a man, for example,

who is a violent drunkard
who is a continual fornicator
who deliberately fails to provide for her and her children
who abuses her and debases her dignity
who fails to exercise his prerogatives as head of the house (which is the literal meaning of "husband"), and so fails to provide the family with proper leadership and priestly covering.

A woman may, of course, choose (for many reasons) to stay with such a man; but nothing in scripture compels her to do so.

ii.  When a husband seeks to assert authority over his wife in matters of religion and conscience, then she is not only not obliged to obey him, she is in fact obliged to disobey him. In all cases she should obey God rather than man. No husband can rightly compel his wife to commit a crime, or to engage in sin, or to separate herself from the church, or to engage in amusements or activities that are repugnant to her.

In such circumstances, when she has exhausted every avenue of loving persuasion and gentle example, only to find him still obdurate in tyranny, she is fully entitled to take steps to free herself from him. But in any case she dare not obey him in preference to obedience to God. (See De 13:6-10; Mt 19:29; Lu 14:26; Ac 4:19-20.

7. There is a peculiar imbalance in many discussions on the relationship between husband and wife. Frequently the emphasis falls on the duty of the wife to obey far more heavily than on the duty of the husband to love. But Paul avoids that chauvinistic error. In Ep 5:21-33 he devotes twice as much space to the husband's duty as he does to the wife's. The fact is, if the husband is indeed the head of the house, then his is the greater responsibility. It is more incumbent upon him to obey the command of God than it is upon his wife to obey his command.

And the command of God to the man is absolute: "Husbands, love your wives" (vs. 25).

He does not say, love her if she is lovely, love her if she submits to you, love her if she is good to you, and the like. He does not say, you need not love her if she fails in these things. He simply says, love her, without qualification; love her in submission to Christ; love her as Christ loves the church; love her sacrificially; love her as you love yourself; love her, nourish her, cherish her, as Christ does the church.

It should be noticed that the emphasis in scripture is not one of rights but of duties.

Hence the wife should not be demanding her rights from her husband, but rather so loving him and submitting to him that he will joyfully give her her rights and much more beside.

A man who is truly and deeply loved by a good and submissive wife, will not usually respond with arrogance and selfishness. On the contrary, he is more prone to feel a kind of awe, of humility, of wonderment that his wife should so elevate him. Does she not know his blemishes more than any person? In the presence of such love, how can he do other than remain wholly true to her, and give her the highest Honour? (Pr 31:28-31).

Likewise, the husband should not demand that his wife submit to him. If he has to demand submission then love has flown and the happiness of the family is broken.

Scripture does not say to the husband, command your wife to obey; on the contrary, he is told only to love her and honour her. Nor does scripture say to the wife, command your husband to love you; on the contrary, she is told only to love him and obey him. The word about wifely submission is not spoken to men, but to women. The word about husbandly love is not spoken to women but to men. Yet all too often it is the men who seize the word about submission, and the women who seize the word about love. This reverses the intention of scripture, panders to human ego, and brings discord and conflict.

So the woman is to submit, whether or not her husband loves her; and the man is to love, whether or not his wife submits to him.

But if he does so love her exclusively, as Christ loved the church and gave himself up for her, and if he does cherish her dearly, honouring her and giving himself to her, then he may expect that his wife will joyfully abandon herself to him and gladly place herself under his headship.

Now let me conclude with a famous passage from that wonderful old commentator, Matthew Henry -

> "Adam was first formed, then Eve (1 Ti 2:13), and
> she was made of the man, and for the man (1 Co

11:8-9), all which are urged there as reasons for the humility. modesty, silence, and submissiveness of that sex in general, and particularly the subjection and reverence which wives owe their own husbands. Yet man being made last of the creatures, as the best and most excellent of all, Eve's being made after Adam, and out of him (Ge 2:21-24), puts an honour upon that sex, as the glory of the man (1 Co 11:7). If man is the head, she is the crown, a crown to her husband, the crown of the visible creation. The man was dust refined, but the woman was dust double-refined, one remove further from the earth ... (She) was 'made of a rib out of the side of Adam,'; not made out of his head to rule over him, nor out of his feet to be trampled upon by him, but out of his side to be equal with him, under his arm to be protected, and near his heart to be beloved."[23]

[23] **Commentary on the Whole Bible**, 6 vols, Marshal, Morgan, and Scott. London. 1965 ed. This quotation is from Vol 1, "Genesis to Deuteronomy", pgs. 19-20.

# CHAPTER SIX

# SUBMISSION IN THE CHURCH

Submission to the leaders of the church is enjoined upon those who are members of the church: "Obey your leaders, and submit to them; for they are keeping watch over your souls, as men who will have to give account" (He 13:17. See also De 12:19; Ph 2:29; 1 Th 5:12,13; 1 Ti 5:17; He 13:7; Mt 16:19; 18:18; Jn 20:23; Ac 20:17,28; 1 Co 16:3,16; Ep 4:11,12; 1 Ti 3:1,2,5; 1 Pe 5:1-3.

Two important principles spring out of those passages -

## THE CHURCH FAMILY

The previous Chapter explained how the domestic Christian family is intended by God to be a place of salvation for its members (Ac 16:31). The husband, the household head, is a kind of priest before God on behalf of his wife and children. He provides a spiritual covering for the family, and the grace of God should flow to its members through him.

In a godly, well-structured home this ideal is often achieved. Yet the best of families may sometimes fail to attain this ideal, and there are many families where it is not even attempted, or where the presence of an unbelieving spouse makes its attainment impossible.

Further, this concept of the priestly ministry of the husband must be balanced by the concept of the priesthood of every Christian. As every man is finally answerable only to God for his spiritual life, so also is every **woman.** A wife may depend on her husband's spiritual covering only so far. Finally she stands alone before God, as does every human soul, and will be obliged to account personally for her faith and obedience to the divine will.

Thus we are each one of us priests before God; each one of us has direct access into the holiest; we must each one of us yield ultimate obedience to the Holy Spirit alone.

But if the domestic family fails, whether through human infirmity or unbelief, or through sin, accident, or death, we are not left without protection or nurture - for God has given us in the church a larger and tougher family, against which the gates of hell cannot prevail.

Christ and the church become spouse and spiritual family to the unmarried, the divorced, the homeless, and to those who are widowed, or who are married to an unbelieving husband or wife. Within the bosom of the church they find what is lacking in their family. Here there is nurture for their souls, along with Christian society, fellowship, temporal provision, brotherly love, and the free operation of divine grace.

There is, of course, much more in the church than this. Godly and united families need the church as much as divided or widowed families. Married people need the church as much as the unmarried. I am simply emphasising that Christian women in particular, and young people, when they are deprived of the spiritual covering, the headship, which should come to them through a godly home, may find it richly in the church. Thus God provides abundant compensation to the widow, the deserted wife, the woman married to an unbeliever, the spinster, the orphan, the young person with godless parents, and so on.

But the many benefits that the church conveys to its members can be received by them only as they observe a second and more important principle -

## ACCESS COMES THROUGH SUBMISSION

"Rebellion is like the sin of witchcraft" (1 Sa 15:23). It arouses the anger of God. It isolates the soul from the mercy of God. It incurs a heavy penalty. Paul spoke of those in the church who became physically ill, and some of whom had died, because of the displeasure of God (1 Co 11:29-32). It is a fearful thing for a rebellious spirit to fall into the hands of the living God (He 10:26-31).

Peter speaks about those who defy authority in the church. He declares that they are certain to be punished. He describes them as "bold and wilful" and as "waterless springs and mists driven by a storm; for them the nether gloom of darkness has been reserved" (2 Pe 2:9-22; see also Jude 8-16).

It is a serious matter to oppose the authority God has vested in his church. Those who do so cannot expect to retain access to the life that God has also implanted in the church. But to be denied access to that life is to be denied access to Christ, for that life is the life of Christ.

Christ and the church are one. He is the Head, the church is his Body on earth. To relate to Christ the Head without first coming into vital union with his Body is simply impossible. Fusion with the Body combined with submission to the permeating authority of the Head, is the only possible way to union with the life of Christ.

Any person who separates from the Body is separating from the Head. Any person who unites with the Body is uniting with the Head (Ep 4:4, 12-16; Col 2:19).

Rebellion against the church is rebellion against the authority of God within the church, which means against Christ. The life of Christ is discoverable within the church and nowhere else. All whom God desires to save he draws into his church, for outside the church (which means outside of Christ) there is no salvation.

Consider yourself. The life of your body is in your body, and nowhere else. The will of your head is expressed through your body and nowhere else.

Likewise, submission to the church (the Body of Christ on earth) is required of all who desire to know and do the will of God and to experience the life of Christ (the Head of that Body).

Certain specific ideas arise from those general concepts -

## 1.  The Church Is A Theocracy

A)  **Government** in the church is not **democratic** but **theocratic**. Authority in the church arises not from the will of the people, but from the will of God. It does not spring up from "the grass roots", nor is it based on majority opinion. In the church, the Son of God rules.

Hence, one man who speaks according to the will of Christ has more authority than a thousand who vote against him; and God will support that man above the multitude.

However, to say that Christ rules in his church, and that he is the source of authority in the church, raises almost as many questions as it answers. How does Christ hold sway? How can his authority be identified? Who speaks for him? Is each person his own arbiter in this matter?

Ordinarily the authority of God in the church will be expressed through a specific and recognisable channel, and in a regular manner. Christians differ in their ideas about this - ranging all the way from the ultimate authority of a congregational vote to the ultimate authority of an episcopal decree.

It is not my intention to argue here for either concept (the various alternatives in church government will be discussed in a later unit). Here I am concerned simply with the **principle of authority;** and for this purpose it will be enough to affirm that normally the authority of Christ will be expressed through the ministry and oversight God himself has raised up in the church. That is, through what Paul called "the bishops and deacons"; or what various Christians today would call "the pastor and elders", or "the ministry team", or "the presbytery", or "the priesthood", or "the council"; and so on (Ph 1:1; Ac 15:6,23; 20:28; and see also the references at the beginning of this Chapter.)

To these "under-shepherds" (however they may be elected, or appointed, or ordained) the Chief Shepherd has conveyed his authority. To them the members of the church are to submit as they would to Christ himself. To refuse their authority is to refuse the lordship of Christ. No man can call Christ "Lord" who refuses to do what he says, and he says, "obey your leaders and submit to them"!

At this point, many commentators stop. They are concerned only with the authority of the church, and they argue as though this authority is absolute. But I have already indicated that this cannot be so. No earthly power is invested with absolute authority by God - neither husband, parent, church, nor state. Always there are qualifiers; and the authority is valid only when it conforms to these qualifiers.

What then must be present before a Christian becomes obligated to submit to ecclesiastical authority? What brings life to the scriptures about episcopal rule? How can you determine whether the Bible references quoted thus far in this Chapter are applicable to your situation?

Plainly, they speak to those circumstances to which they were addressed; they do not speak to all circumstances. The following modifiers determine the circumstances in which an exercise of authority by the church becomes valid -

## 2. Five Important Modifiers

Before you willingly submit to any authority, you should check that authority's credentials. You are entitled to establish that it does indeed have the authority it claims.

Hence it is incumbent upon Christian people to ascertain whether or not the body to which they are submitting is indeed a true church, that it really does possess authority, and that the areas in which it is seeking to exercise authority are within its scriptural prerogatives.

Unfortunately, many Christians are defaulters in this matter, and they come under the authority of groups

- ♦ which have never qualified as a church, or
- ♦ which have forfeited their church identity, or
- ♦ which seek to exercise an improper control over their people.

But God has given no authority to false claimants! Spurious churches have no rights over the people of God!

So submission to ecclesiastical authority must be modified by five important factors-

## A) Submission Is Required Only To A True Church

You should not submit to a group that has never established its claim to be recognised as a true church; nor should you submit to a church that has departed from true faith and practice, and thus has forfeited its identity.

What is a true church? When does a group of Christians meeting together become transformed into a church?

Jesus said, "Where two or three are gathered in my name, there am I in the midst of them" (Mt 18:20). Some commentators have claimed that this is the simplest expression of a church: a small company of people with Christ in the midst. No doubt that is true - particularly if "church" is given its broadest definition as the "called-out" or "gathered" people of God.

However, a more precise definition cannot allow that merely collecting a few Christians together is sufficient to form a church. Christ is indeed present in every gathering of his people; he promised this, and it is true. **But his presence by itself does not turn that gathering into a church.**

Before any assembly of Christians can rightly be recognised as a church, other factors must be present. Some of those factors are -[24]

### i.  A formal union

To create a recognisable church, the first essential is for a group of Christians to unite themselves formally as a worshipping body. That implies a stated time and place of assembly, a certain degree of structure and order, and an agreed set of principles and practices.

---

[24] In preparing this list I consulted numerous commentators, and made an analysis of the factors each one said were essential to every local church. The list given here is compiled from that analysis. It may be fairly said to represent a wide range of evangelical opinion on the things that are necessary to turn a group of Christians into a church

An informal fellowship of Christians, whether few or many, does not meet that requirement (cp. He 10:23-25; and 1 Co 14:26-33,40).

## ii. Preaching

A fellowship of Christians does not become a church unless that fellowship exists primarily as a forum in which the preaching of the word of God has pre-eminence. A church that gives itself only to prayer and praise, that considers fellowship or even worship to be its primary task, that minimises the preaching office, or that values debate and dialogue above proclamation, has fallen away from its God-given identity.

Christians who come together in formal union, to create a church, should do so with the primary aim of promoting in every way possible the preaching of the word of God. Authority in the church stems from the word of God, especially when it is preached. If preaching decays, then authority will fail with it.

## iii. The sacraments

The sacraments of baptism and holy communion are an integral part of the life of every local church. No true church can exist without at least those two sacraments.

Have you ever realised that there are few things Christ commanded his church to do as a church? He gave numerous instructions to his disciples individually; but to the whole church, acting as the church, he gave very few instructions. Probably the most important are: **preach the word, heal the sick, baptise those who believe, observe holy communion** (Mt 28:18-20; Mk 16:15; Lu 9:1-6; 10:1,9; 1 Co 11:23-26; Ja 5:14-15). Virtually all that he said to the church is comprehended in those four; and of them the greatest is the first: "Go into all the world and preach the gospel to the whole creation."

As I have mentioned just above, a church that has lost confidence in its preaching mandate has sadly lapsed from the high calling God has placed before it.

But word and sacrament are closely linked. Neither of them should be separated from the other. Preaching is vitally important for the sacraments; for it is out of the proclamation of the word of God that authority arises to practise the sacraments. But then the faithful observance of the sacraments indicates that a company of Christians have in fact formed themselves into a church in which the Word can be preached. If the sacraments are absent, then no church is present; if the word is absent, then the sacraments have no validity. Both are essential for a properly formed church.

### iv. <u>Oversight</u>

Since a church consists initially of a group of Christians who have come into formal union as a worshipping body, it follows that a pattern of oversight must be established.

Various churches have adopted different methods of government, both at local and national levels. But each system is an extension or adaptation of the basic pattern given in the NT.

The early churches, we are told, were governed by "bishops and deacons". Whatever else that may mean, it certainly shows -

      a.   that God has established levels of authority within the church; he has not left it leaderless.

      b.   that the leaders of the church are people who fulfil certain conditions, who possess certain abilities, and who are recognised by the congregation as being gifted and chosen by God to serve him in the church.

      c.   that these people comprise a divinely ordained oversight within the church, and they are the channels through which God will both reveal his will for the church and manifest his authority over it.

     d.   that a gathering of Christians cannot be truly described as a church until this divinely appointed oversight has been raised up from among, or brought to, the people.

     e.   that no matter what method is adopted to recognise and appoint this oversight, once appointed, it should be accepted by the people as representing the authority of God within the church.

## v.  Discipline

The "bishops and deacons" (that is, the oversight of the local church) are given responsibility by God to rule the church in his name.  Responsibility means authority, and the ultimate source of authority is discipline.  If the sanctions of the overseers cannot be enforced, or if the members of the church refuse to acknowledge them, then the rule of God in the church is destroyed.  Thus the existence of effective discipline reveals a true church (cp.  De 17:10-13; Mt 16:19; 18:15-18; 1 Co 4:19,21; 16:22; 2 Co 13:1,2,10; 2 Th 3:6,14,15; 1 Ti 1:19,20; 5:1,2,19,20; 6:3-5; Tit 1:13; 2:15; 3:10,11).

## vi.  Pastoral care

There is no true church unless a programme of faithful and compassionate pastoral care has been established in the congregation. Jesus, that Good Shepherd of the sheep, does not leave his flock defenceless before the wolves.  The care of the sheep is one of the imperatives of the church (Ac 20:28).

Those, then, are the factors that turn a company of Christians into a church.  To such a local church God has imparted his own authority.  To refuse to submit to your church, when it is established in scriptural order, is to resist, not the church, but God.

On the other hand, to anything less than such a scripturally ordered church you have no obligation to submit.  God has not given his authority to all that men might choose to call a church.  He has given authority to, and requires submission to, only those assemblies that fulfil the pattern given in scripture.

## B) Church Overseers Must Be Theocratic, Not Autocratic

Church overseers are forbidden to act as though they were lords over the flock of God. Any such domineering authority may rightly be resisted by the people of God (1 Pe 5:1-4).

By gentle example, by patient love, and only as a last resort, by stern rebuke, the under-shepherds must nurture the sheep. They should be men of tears as they keep watch over the souls of the people given into their care. They have no authority of their own. They represent only God's authority. They speak with strength only when they speak his word. They act with power only when they are doing his will.

The true church is a theocracy (ruled by a gracious God), not an autocracy (ruled by proud men). Any man who, by his humble life, his merciful demeanour, his close walk with God, and his adherence to scripture, proves that his words may be taken as the word of God, has a right to command me. But such a man will do so with kindness, compassion, and forbearance, and I will gladly yield obedience to him.[25] But an autocrat, who speaks out of pride, who is insensitive to the Holy Spirit, who evidently speaks his own will, not the will of God, I not only **may, but must, resist**.

However, since the kingdom of God is based on good order, any resistance to properly constituted authority is a very serious matter. Lawlessness is anathema to God. More often than not it is better to yield to mistakenly exercised authority than to oppose it. In most instances, you can place the matter in God's hand, having confidence that he will eventually correct what is wrong.

---

[25] An exception to the law of submission could occur if one has compelling reasons for believing that a godly spiritual leader is mistaken in a particular instance, and that error is serious enough to warrant disobedience

But I cannot make that an absolute rule. There are plainly cases where grave error is involved, or where to obey will demonstrably cause greater harm than to resist. In such cases, protest, or even a refusal to obey, may become imperative. There are times, then, when a congregation, even though it believes a leader to be mistaken, should yield to him, knowing that if he is wrong the Lord of the church will in time rectify the error. They should not be eager to undermine the leader's authority, not to grieve the Holy Spirit by developing a rebellious spirit.

But there are other times when submission may cause greater disorder than resistance, and in such cases it is right to resist.

The writer to the Hebrews says we should submit to those godly men who are true shepherds of the sheep, because they are "keeping watch" over our souls (He 13:17). They keep watch because they know that one day "they will have to give an account" to God of the faithfulness with which they discharged their duty. If, says the apostle, they can give that account with joy, because we obeyed them gladly and submitted to them in the Lord, that will be of great advantage to us. But if they give account sadly, because we were lawless and rebellious, and resisted all their efforts to discipline and train us in Christ, then, he says, "that will be of no advantage" to us.

In conformity with these principles, then, every Christian should look for a church with a genuinely theocratic oversight, and happily place themselves under the protective care and discipline of that church.

## C) Church Overseers Must Themselves Be Under Authority

You may well have been wondering: if the overseers rule the church, who rules the overseers? How do we stop them from becoming autocratic? How do we determine whether they are theocratic?

The test is simple. Those who wish to exercise authority must be under authority (cp. Mt 8:9; and see also Jn 13:3-17; Ja 3:1; Ac 20:35; Ro 12:10,16; 1 Co 9:19-22; Ga 5:13; 6:1-2; Ph 2:2-5; 1 Pe 5:5).

The overseers of the church should themselves be seen to be men and women who can humbly receive rebuke from the least member of the church, who give heed to one another, who are respectful toward the congregation of God, and who walk tenderly before the Lord.

### D) <u>The Priesthood Of Each Believer Must Be Maintained</u>

See Ex 19:6; Is 61:65; 1 Pe 2:9; Re 1:6; 5:10; 20:6.

Those references state in the clearest terms that every Christian has priestly status in the eyes of God. We need no intermediary, save Christ, the great High Priest, to stand between us and God. We are not required to approach God through a second party. As anointed priests each one of us has direct access into the holiest place (He 10:19-23; plus many other references to our right to come directly to God in prayer in the name of Christ; eg. Ro 5:1-5; 1 Ti 2:5-6; He 4:14-16; and so on).

In this conferring of priesthood there is no distinction between clergy and laity.

But what about those churches where it is a matter of custom or of convenience to call their spiritual leader a "priest"? If it means only that he is the minister of God to the people, then the title accurately expresses his scriptural role.

But if it is taken to mean that he is the minister of the people to God, then it expresses a usurpation of authority and of prerogative that is against scripture.

I need no man save Christ to represent me to God. I will concede to no man a greater freedom of access to God than I have myself. None can more boldly enter the sanctuary by the blood of Jesus. None can more confidently draw near to the throne of God, nor find richer mercy, nor discover more prevalent grace in time of need. And of course, if you have put your trust in Christ, you too may take the same bold stand. Neither priest, nor pastor, nor bishop, nor minister, nor any other dignitary, has any better right than that of the humblest believer to come into the Father's presence and to receive his richest blessings.

For that reason I dare not allow any person or church to impose a fetter upon my soul, nor to imprison my conscience. I listen with humility and respect to all that good and godly men say to me. I ponder their advice and counsel with care. I joyfully submit to the authority of the church. But at all times I preserve my final freedom of conscience and the right to receive instruction directly from God. Ultimately, you and I must answer to God alone, not to man or church, for what we have believed and wrought.

So I submit to the church because usually in its voice I hear the voice of God. But if this ever ceases to be so, then I must obey God rather than man. The command of the Holy Spirit is more urgent than any other. That is the sense of John's word: "I write this to you about those who would deceive you; **but the anointing which you received from him abides in you, and you have no need that any one should teach you;** as his anointing teaches you about everything, and is true, and is no lie, just as it has taught you, abide in him" (1 Jn 2:26-27).

There is a breathtaking daring about that passage. John is bold and unequivocal in his insistence that the final arbiter in any dispute of conscience must be the **word of God taught by the Holy Spirit.** He will allow no man to be the infallible interpreter of God's word to him. And he insists that his readers should stand just as free from all human coercion. Each Christian is personally responsible before God for the doctrines he believes, and for the deeds he performs. No man or church should be elevated to a place of inerrancy. No ecclesiastical authority has power from God to command any Christian to act against his own conscience, or against his deep sense of what God is saying to him. There is a point at which the Christian must assert his liberty of conscience, his freedom from the authority of a mistaken church, his independent right of direct priestly access to God.

Plainly there is peril in asserting such things, and many spiritual leaders have tried to impose much tighter restraints upon their followers.

But to accept such restraints simply betrays lack of confidence in the effective priesthood of each believer, in the validity of personal prayer, and in the ability of the Holy Spirit to guide the servants of God successfully.

> *John said, "You have no need that any one should teach you (for) his anointing teaches you about everything ... You have been anointed by the Holy One, and you know everything" (vs. 27,20).*

By "everything" he cannot mean all forms of knowledge (history, science, art, etc.). The sense is rather, everything to do with the will of God for your life, or all that you personally need to know about the divine purpose - those things, the Holy Spirit is able to teach you.

But how will he teach you? Independently of any means? Without the use of scripture? Employing no other teacher?

Can you reasonably ignore all other sources of information and guidance?

It cannot be imagined that John intended to advocate such an extreme view. When he said "you have no need that any one should teach you" he could not have meant that you can dispense with all human teachers. After all, he was himself giving instruction to the church when he wrote his letter!

A teaching ministry is part of God's gift to the church - see Mt 28:19; Ro 12:7; 1 Co 12:28; Ep 4:11; 1 Ti 3:2; 4:11; 6:2; 2 Ti 2:2,24; He 5:12.

So it is evident that the Holy Spirit does usually guide us through the counsel of mature and godly teachers. Only the strongest reasons should cause any Christian to ignore the teachers under whom God has placed him. But when those strong reasons exist, says John, then we must heed the voice of the Holy Spirit above all others. You own conscience, directed by the Holy Spirit, must be for you the final arbiter of right and wrong.

A major safeguard in this process is the word of God. The leaders of the church, and the people, are alike bound by scripture. No voice, whether of man or spirit, that is discordant with scripture, can be recognised as the voice of God. **All things must be tested by their conformity to scripture** (Is 8:20, AV; 1 Th 5:19-20; 1 Jn 4:1; Re 22:18-19; etc.)

## E) <u>The Church Has A Limited Competence</u>

It ought to be self-evident that the church has authority only within its own sphere of competence. Yet churches and spiritual leaders have often seized, and people have often encouraged them to seize, much more extensive powers.

On matters of faith and morals, the church (when it is rightly interpreting scripture), speaks with the authority of God. But in all other matters it lacks divine inspiration. It has been given no authority by God to interfere in the private lives of people. It has no right to instruct people on matters that are merely domestic, social, cultural, or political, unless some law of God is being clearly violated. It ought not to trespass on areas that are a matter of personal choice or opinion.

Hence I would tolerate no control by the church over where I live, how my home is structured, what employment I choose, how my leisure is spent, what literature, art, or music I prefer, what recreations I enjoy, or what political views I hold. Those all lie beyond the competence of the church - unless, as I have just said, my words or actions contradict some part of scripture.

The primary responsibility the church has in such matters is to teach spiritual principles, the laws of faith and righteousness, and to train the people into mature Christians, so that when faced with an ethical choice they will choose that which best reflects Christian values and standards. But a church that seeks to make such decisions for its people, refusing them liberty of conscience, is simply creating a pattern of legalism that will bind the people instead of liberating them. Against all such legalises, Paul sets the admonition: "For freedom Christ has set us free; stand fast therefore, and do not submit again to a yoke of slavery" (Ga 5:1).

# SECTION THREE

# LIVING
# WITH YOUR
# GOD

# CHAPTER SEVEN

# SUBMISSION IN SOCIETY

That remarkable man Watchman Nee wrote a book called "Spiritual Authority"[26]. You may be able to obtain a copy of it. If you do, you will probably not agree with all that you find in it, and you might even react strongly to some of Watchman Nee's claims. In that book, as in some of his others, he tends toward an extreme view. But his powerful and invigorating writing will nonetheless provoke you to new levels of understanding!

Some of what you will find in this Lesson is drawn from Watchman Nee's "Spiritual Authority", although in a modified and shortened form, and I am happy to acknowledge my debt to him. Those who have read his book will see his mark in several of the following paragraphs.

## THE PRINCIPLE OF AUTHORITY

*"Once God has spoken; twice have I heard this: that power belongs to God" (Ps 62:11)*

### 1. Authority Is The Basis Of God's Dominion

God has two great attributes: authority and power. **Power describes the acts of God**, the things he does by his limitless strength. **But authority describes the very nature of God**, the

---

[26]  Published by Christian Fellowship Publishers Inc.; New York; 1972

base upon which he performs his mighty works. Thus authority is more fundamental than power.

Power that is exercised without proper authority is tyranny or lawlessness. But that is never true of God. His authority is derived from his eternal nature and is an expression of his office as Creator and Sustainer of all things. Whatever he does, he does with authority. He cannot act outside his authority.

Authority is fundamental to God, even more fundamental than power, which is simply an expression of his authority.

Therefore, to sin against the authority of God is to rebel deeply against God himself. And that is true wherever God's authority is found, whether in direct or delegated form. So, if you meet the authority of God in scripture, **it must be yielded to.** If you meet it through those who represent God in the home, school, office, factory, shop, government, or church, it must be yielded to. There can be no exceptions. Divine authority demands submission.

It is certain that the Lord God will brook no resistance to his authority, no matter where that authority is found, nor how many times it has been delegated. Rebellion will find its punishment.

Ultimately all true authority (as distinct from usurped tyranny), whether it is found in heaven or on earth, stems from God. Indeed, it could be said that authority is the most important thing in the universe. Nothing can function properly if authority is not understood and accepted. Nobody can truly serve God who does not understand the use of authority, in the home, in the church, and in society at large.

## 2. <u>Authority Is The Great Controversy</u>

Across the ages the great controversy has been: who shall have authority? This conflict is described in the words Christ spoke to Paul: "I send you to open their eyes, that they may turn from darkness to light, and from the power of Satan to God" (Ac 26:18).

The conflict is between darkness and light, between Satan and God. **The prize is ultimate authority.** However, the issue is never in doubt. The kingdom of God will inevitably prevail. Nonetheless the contest continues., and will do so until Christ comes.

Who is Satan? Scripture suggests that he is a mighty spirit who was cast out of heaven because of his vaunting pride and rebellion against God (cp. Is 14:12-14; Ez 28:12-15). "Satan" means "Adversary". And he has ever been the Adversary of God and of the people of God. We are at war with Satan, and he hates us, because we attribute authority to God, and we have been brought out of the kingdom of darkness and into the kingdom of God's Son (Col 1:13).

The principle of Satan is **rebellion**. This must be deeply recognised. All lawful authority in the universe is ultimately God's authority. To rebel against lawful authority, wherever it is found, is to follow the principle of Satan, it is to enter into an alliance with the kingdom of darkness.

The chief characteristic of Satan, and of all who serve him, wittingly or unwittingly, is rebellion. How sad it is to see this principle of Satan operating so often in the church. There are many people who appear to stand with Christ in doctrine, yet in reality they live by this principle of Satan - they are not submissive in their spirits, they "reject authority", they unhesitatingly "speak evil of dignities", they are "grumblers, malcontents, following their own passions, loudmouthed boasters ... bold and wilful" (Jude 8,16; 2 Pe 3:10).

Such people often think they are serving God, they are proud of their independence, they think they have a zeal for truth, but in reality they are slaves to the satanic principle of rebellion. Such people cause Satan no terror, no matter how well they may preach, for are they not at heart his friends? But he trembles when he sees the servants of God properly under authority, for they are then in true alliance with the kingdom of God.

To know the protection of God's authority, we must be subject to it, in all of its various expressions - whether direct or indirect, through society, church, or home. Remember again that **all lawful authority is backed by God's authority: "Let every person be subject to the governing authorities. For there is no authority except from God, and those that exist have been instituted by God. Therefore he who resists the authorities resists what God has appointed, and those who resist will incur judgment"** (Ro 13:1-2).

It should be noted that this passage and many others clearly distinguish between the authority and the person behind the authority. Whether the person is of good character or bad, whether he is godly or ungodly, if he is exercising lawful authority he must be obeyed. When you meet with proper authority you should deal with that, not with the person behind it. You should not examine the person first before you decide whether to obey or disobey the authority. That attitude draws people into the principle of Satan.

# THE PRINCIPLE OF OBEDIENCE

## 1. Obedience Is Righteousness

A) See 1 Sa 15:17-31. Nothing is so important as doing exactly what God asks, even if that includes doing nothing (which for many people is the hardest obedience of all). Saul did more than God commanded him to do. He offered sacrifices he was not authorised to offer. Samuel rebuked him: "Has the Lord as great delight in burnt offerings and sacrifices, as in obeying the voice of the Lord? Behold, to obey is better than sacrifice ... For rebellion is as the sin of divination, and stubbornness is as iniquity and idolatry." Saul's wilful spirit cost him his throne, his kingdom, and his life.

Yet for all that, Samuel was careful not to belittle Saul's lawful authority. He rebuked the king in private. And when Saul pleaded for Samuel to maintain his public honour, the prophet did so: "(Saul) said, 'I have sinned; yet honour me now before the elders of my people and before Israel, and return with me, that I may worship the Lord your God.' So Samuel turned back after Saul."

Samuel knew the principles of authority and submission. The prophet spoke boldly when he had authority to speak; he obeyed graciously when obedience was called for.

B) See how Paul despised a man, yet yielded instantly to the authority of the office that man held - Ac 23:1-5. Despite his own high authority as an apostle of Christ, Paul acknowledged that scripture required him to show all respect to the leader of Israel. He quoted Ex 22:28, "You shall not revile God, nor curse a ruler of your people."

Notice the inference of this command: to curse a lawful ruler is in fact the same as reviling God, for the ruler has his office and authority from God. By contrast with Paul, how many there are in the church, who do not hesitate on a slight pretext to speak critically and maliciously of their leaders!

C) The most important place where we meet God's authority is in the church. There we learn submission to God as we obey the injunction to "be subject to each other" (Ep 5:21). Many in the church have not learned this submission. That is true even of many who are seemingly very busy in the work of God. But their efforts are worthless (like the sacrifices King Saul offered) because they are placing their own works against the will of God (Mt 7:21-22).

We really have only one important task: discover the will of God and do it. To do more than he asks is presumption; to do less than he asks is evasion; and both spring out of the principle of Satan, rebellion. It is enough for each one of us to be what God wants us to be, and to do what he want us to do, whether little or much.

## 2. **Examples Of Disobedience**

A) Adam and Eve (Ge 2:16-17; 3:1-6)

Notice how God first put all things under the authority of Adam and Eve, but then placed those two under his authority. Only those who are under authority may rightly exercise authority. Because Adam and Eve shrugged off the authority of God they quickly lost their own authority. The earth and its creatures were no longer submissive to them.

Adam and Eve both failed to recognise authority: she would not accept Adam's authority over her, so she acted independently and sinned; and in his turn, he failed to exercise authority over her, so he stepped down to her and shared her sin.

To rebel against God's representative authority (as Eve did), and to fail to exercise a given authority (as Adam did), are both acts of rebellion against God; they reflect the principle of Satan.

We must kill self-will. Many of our furious activities are camouflage for deep-rooted disobedience. We are restless and anxious because we are not in God's will. Thus Adam and Eve laboured to fashion garments for themselves, to smother their sense of nakedness.

But the "last Adam", Jesus, set a very different example. He lived quietly for 30 years, obedient to his parents (Lu 2:51-52), not fretful, but biding his Father's time. Even when the time came, he was content to work for only three years, scrupulous to do his Father's will in everything, great and small.

Thus Christ has left us with an example of gracious submission (Mt 11:28,29; 12:19-20; 1 Pe 2:21-23). But Adam has left us with a legacy of rebellion. Everyone wants to do his own thing. Everyone thinks he knows better than God. We need to be delivered from this, and to learn that only obedience is righteousness.

Adam ate the fruit of "the knowledge of good and evil". He wanted to make up his own mind what was right and wrong, to usurp the divine prerogative of determining what is righteous. But God wanted him only to obey. The issues of right and wrong should have been left in God's hands. Now man is cursed with a burden he cannot carry, and he lives in confusion, with a warped and unbalanced conscience.

We who are Christians, however, can thank God that he has substantially delivered us from Satan's folly. If we take upon ourselves the mind of Christ, and come under authority as we should be, then we will be able once again to will and to work for God's good pleasure (Ph 2:3-5, 12-13; Ro 12:1-2).

Our privilege, then, is to know each authority that is above us, in every department of life, and to submit to that authority. And this is especially true within the church. Whenever a few Christians come together, a spiritual order will soon appear. That order develops in several stages

- ◆ it begins with the whole company submitting itself heartily to the authority of Christ, the Head.

- ◆ it should then continue with each member giving submission to the delegated authority of Christ; that is, to the spiritual overseers God establishes in the church.

- ◆ then those to whom authority has been delegated should be bold and wise in the exercise of their responsibilities.

Thus good order is established, and the church can flourish under the authority and favour of God, for the Holy Spirit is never the author of confusion, but always of peace (1 Co 14:33).

## B) The Rebellion of Ham (Ge 9:20-27)

Because Noah had disgraced himself Ham felt that he was free to scorn his father's authority; but he was punished for that rebellion by a sentence of slavery.

Ultimately, the one who is not subject to authority always becomes a slave to one who is subject to authority. The law-abiding will in the end always defeat the lawless. God is against the rebellious; but he supports those who act within authority.

Special blessing was promised to the two sons who stayed under authority. Shem was greatly favoured by God, and from him Christ was descended. Japheth inherited the blessing of Shem. Ham remained depressed for many generations. Every person who desires to serve God must, like Japheth, meet authority. No one can serve God in the spirit of lawlessness.

## C) Nadab And Abihu (Le 10:1-2)

Because their father was authorised to offer incense, these two men felt that they also had a right to do so. They arrogated to themselves an authority that did not belong to them, so a fearful penalty was exacted from them.

That incident reinforces the principle that all divine service must be initiated by God, and performed under authority. Many people, sadly, are deluded by the fact that "unholy fire" and "holy fire" look the same to man; but God is not deceived. To act independently of God's direct or delegated authority will invite his displeasure. Whatever we do must be done within authority.

## D) Aaron And Miriam (Nu 12:1-16)

All lawful authority represents the authority of God. To speak rashly, or to act rashly, against representative authority is to risk provoking the wrath of God. Be careful how you speak and whom you challenge!

That principle functions strongly in the church.

Because spiritual authority is not attained by natural effort or skill, because it arises from a divine mandate, rebellion in the church is seen as direct rebellion against God. For this reason, Moses knew he did not have to defend himself. He knew that Miriam was actually attacking God, and that God would act in defence of his own authority.

Those who are under divine authority do not have to rush to their own defence. They have no sense of insecurity. They do not feel threatened by attack. They are content, as Moses was, to leave the matter in God's hands (cp. Ro 12:14-21).

I am not saying that they should take no action to stop the mouths of slanderers, nor to prevent division in the church. They most certainly should act - as Moses did - for it would be quite irresponsible to allow evil people, without restraint or penalty, to do as they please.

But whatever action is taken must be free of malice; there should be no hint of human vengeance; it should accord with scripture; it should be done in the authority of God; it should be tempered by the fruit of the Spirit (Ga 5:22-24).

Moses had an immense authority. He was given the highest honour, of speaking to God "mouth to mouth, clearly, and not in dark speech," and he was privileged to behold "the form of the Lord" (vs. 6-8).

But that extraordinary status did not puff Moses up with pride; on the contrary, he was "very meek, more than all men that were on the face of the earth" (vs.3).

God-given authority does not create arrogance. A person who is proud in his authority creates a suspicion that the authority is usurped; it certainly shows that he is not under authority, that he is motivated by the principle of Satan (which is rebellion), rather than by the principle of God (which is submission).

The story suggests that Miriam and Aaron may have had a legitimate complaint against Moses in the matter of his marriage to the Cushite woman. Does it mean that no voice can ever be raised against the faults or mistakes of a leader? Hardly! The sin of Miriam and Aaron did not lie in their protest against Moses, but in the manner of it.

As an older sister, Miriam could have approached Moses on a different basis, and she may well have gained God's support. Her fault was public slander of Moses' spiritual authority, and of rebellion against that authority.

But the mistake Moses may have made in his choice of wife was not sufficient excuse for such serious action.

Likewise, within the church, a pattern has been given for dealing with those who are at fault, whether leaders or people - Mt 18:15-18; 1 Ti 5:19.

### E) <u>Korah, Dathan, Abiram, And On (Nu 16:1-50)</u>

That passage describes a double revolt: the people rebelled against both the **ecclesiastical authority of Aaron** and the **political authority of Moses**. The basis of the revolt was a spurious democratic right: "You have gone too far! For all the congregation are holy, every one of them, and the Lord is among them; why then do you exalt yourselves above the assembly of the Lord" (vs. 3).

There was a sense in which that claim was true. The whole nation was indeed "a kingdom of priests", holy to the Lord. But this did not give the people the right to defy the levels of authority God had set in the nation.

That same spirit of rebellion is still abroad today. There are still those who misappropriate scripture to justify an attitude of wilful independence, of insubordination, of action against lawful authority.

Korah and his Levite associates led the ecclesiastical revolt against the spiritual authority of Aaron. The result? Two hundred and fifty of them were slain by fire.

Dathan and Abiram led the political revolt against the governmental authority of Moses. The result? They and their families were swallowed into a crevasse.

Notice the charge Moses laid against Korah and the Levites. He accused them of refusing to accept the rank God had given them, of coveting more than the Lord had apportioned to them. He made it plain that they were in fact fighting God, not Aaron –

> *"Hear now, you sons of Levi: is it too small a thing for you that the God of Israel has separated you from the congregation of Israel, to bring you near to himself, to do service in the tabernacle of the Lord ... and would you seek the priesthood also? Therefore it is against the Lord that you and all your company have gathered together ... "*

John the Baptist (Lu 3:10-14) and Paul (1 Co 7:17-24) both stress that people should accept with contentment their station in life, secure in the knowledge that God has ordered all things in harmony with his own wisdom.

Now that does not prevent proper ambition, nor block the way to achieving lawfully a higher status in life. Paul, for example, approved of slaves gaining their freedom if an opportunity to do so came their way (vs. 21). But if no opportunity presented itself, then they were to be content with divine providence and so make use of their present condition to serve God.

Incessant dissatisfaction, perpetual frustration, continual restlessness, a deep inner malaise - those are not the mark of a godly spirit; they are more indicative of resentment against the providence of God. They reflect the principle of Satan more than the principle of God. A godly spirit will eagerly use every opportunity for personal advancement and betterment; it will seek to develop its potential to the full; but it will do so without envy or malice, without any sense of rebellion, and with glad submission to the overall sovereignty of God.

In the matter of Korah, notice again how Moses took what steps were proper for him to take personally; but he was content to leave the final outcome in God's hands. He sought divine, rather than human, vindication. We should follow the same example.

If it is asked why God's judgment was so pitiless on those four men, their followers, and their families, remember that rebellion is the principle of Satan. It could not be tolerated so early in the nation's experience.

Yet God's dealings are hardly less harsh, even if less evident, today. Observation of life shows that rebellion, particularly in the church, but also in the larger society, still attracts a harsh penalty. God still works to sustain lawful authority, and to overthrow those who revolt against his rule.

A further spiritual principle is discovered in the affair of Korah. Despite the death of the rebellious leaders, on the next day the entire congregation moved against Moses and Aaron (vs. 41 ff.). How could that be? How could they dare to revolt again so soon?

You need to recognise that knowledge of authority must come by divine revelation. The people were able to discredit the fire, the crevasse, the plague, as accidents of nature; in any case, brute force rarely persuades anyone to change his mind. Force may be necessary to vindicate righteousness and uphold authority, but it has no skill to convert the unruly.

But see what happened after the plague had run its course - 17:1-12. The budding rod of Aaron, with its blossoms and almonds, may be seen as a type of divine revelation. What the awful terror of the sundered earth could not achieve, was wrought by the fragrant proclamation of the flowering rod. It spoke a lovely message of pardon and life. The people saw it, were persuaded by the Spirit, and believed.

May that same Spirit graciously and supernaturally reveal to each one of us the place he has appointed for us, the authority we are under, and the authority we are called to exercise. So will God be glorified, and his work the more perfectly done.

### 3. <u>Two Good Examples</u>

#### A) <u>David</u>

See 1 Sa 24:4-6; 26:9-11; 2 Sa 1:14.

Although David knew that God had anointed him to be Israel's king, he declined to seize the throne from Saul by rebellion. He refused to touch the man who was still (so long as he remained on the throne) "the Lord's anointed".

How careful we should be not to act improperly against those to whom God has given authority!

David knew (a) he could not serve God if he was not subject to authority; (b) it was God's prerogative to remove Saul; (c) no amount of zeal or consecration on David's part could cover the sin of rebellion. His example is still relevant.

David was not subject to the man Saul, but rather to the anointing of God which, despite Saul's great personal failure, still belonged to him as king .

This total commitment by David to God's authority, both direct and delegated, is exemplified by his steadfast refusal to make war against the king, and by his stern judgment on the young Amalekite (2 Sa 1:6-16).

### B) Christ

See He 5:8-9; Ph 2:5-11.

Authority in the world was destroyed by the Fall. It had to be re-established; and this could be done only by finding an obedient servant, for true authority cannot exist apart from willing submission.

Notice that once authority has to be enforced its character is changed. Disorder has been introduced. Authority becomes power; it may even become tyranny. God did not intend his world to be ruled by power, but by authority. If everybody recognised authority and cheerfully submitted to it the world would be transformed. That happy condition will be universally established when Christ returns. But even now it should be seen in the church. Recognition of authority must surely begin with the people of God.

Christ resolved to become the willing Servant through whom true authority would be restored, first to the church, then to the world. He did this by a double humbling of himself: he emptied himself of his divinity; and he abased himself in his humanity. He stepped first from heaven to earth, and then from earth to the cross. He learned obedience by the things he suffered.

It was so easy for him to defend himself against his enemies. He could have called on legions of angels! But he submitted himself to wicked men in obedience to the will of God.

By his obedience, Christ laid the foundation for re-instatement of God's authority and for rebuilding the kingdom of God. This had to be done in heaven as well as on earth, for the authority of God was challenged by both groups of beings who had been created to live beneath his throne: angels and men. But now, by his obedient life, and by his death, resurrection, and ascension, Christ has ensured that the authority of God will again be acknowledged throughout the universe.

It is inescapable, then, that all who seek to follow Christ, and to belong to the kingdom of God, will place themselves under authority.

# DELEGATED AUTHORITY

## 1. Faith And Obedience

In almost every place where the Bible mentions "faith" it also mentions "obedience". The one is finally impossible without the other. The old song is true when it says that we must both "Trust and obey!" True believers **can also be called obeyers!**

God not only calls us to receive his life through faith, but to maintain his authority through obedience. Without obedience, without submission to authority, we undermine the kingdom of God and re-introduce the kingdom of darkness.

Obedience should exist at three levels

- ♦ to the authority of God.
- ♦ to the authority of scripture.
- ♦ to delegated authority.

God places equal importance on all three of those levels (when they are functioning properly), so that to rebel against any of them is to rebel against all. All such rebellion follows the principle of Satan.

People have difficulty with authority, especially in the third area, namely ....

## 2. Delegated Authority

Many people are able to obey only a person they like, or of whom they approve, which shows that they have not understood the meaning of authority. To those who know authority, even a slight disobedience to lawful command will fill them with the shame of rebellion - as David's heart smote him because he had cut off a piece of Saul's robe (1 Sa 24:5).

But those who have not seen authority have no idea how rebellious they are. We need to pray that God will give us submissive hearts, and eyes open to see where his authority lies.

If the church refuses to accept God's authority, then God has no way to establish his kingdom. His way is to establish the principle of authority, first in the Lord Jesus Christ, then in the church, and finally in the world.

The first part of this Section discussed delegated authority in the home and in the church. I want to look now at delegated authority in the world.

Paul is emphatic in his assertion that all lawful authority is ordained by God, and that it represents God's own authority. **I have quoted this passage already, but it deserves repetition:**

> *"Let every person be subject to the governing authorities. For there is no authority except from God, and those that exist have been instituted by God. Therefore he who resists the authorities resists what God has appointed, and those who*

> *resist will incur judgment ... (the authority) is*
> *God's servant for your good ... he is the servant of*
> *God to execute his wrath on the wrongdoer.*
> *Therefore one must be subject, not only to avoid*
> *God's wrath but also for the sake of conscience ...*
> *the authorities are ministers of God" (Ro 13:1-7).*

That passage is surprising to us when we remember that Paul was not describing a democratic government such as we enjoy, but the Roman dictatorship. In many places it was a corrupt and decadent government. Yet scripture leaves no doubt that the government of imperial Rome was as much the servant of God as the government of a modern democracy. So long as Rome maintained order, and punished wrongdoers, the church could find no grounds on which to foment revolution.

Peter wrote just as emphatically as Paul:

> *"Be subject for the Lord's sake to every human*
> *institution, whether it be to the emperor as supreme,*
> *or to governors as sent by him to punish those who*
> *do wrong and to praise those who do right ... Live*
> *as free men, yet without using your freedom as a*
> *pretext for evil; but live as servants of God.*
> *Honour all men. Love the brotherhood. Fear God.*
> *Honour the emperor. Servants, be submissive to*
> *your masters with all respect, not only to the kind*
> *and gentle but also to the overbearing" (1 Pe 2:13-*
> *18).*

There is a recognition of authority in that passage that sits very uncomfortably on the spirit of modern man. To respect an "overbearing" employer or government officer is not easy! Yet Peter's demand in unequivocal: "be submissive to them with all respect."

Consider also the "emperor" to whom Peter referred. It was Nero, one of the most despicable and barbaric men who has ever occupied a throne. Yet Peter does not change his insistence that Christian citizens must honour Nero's office, and that Christian slaves must respect even a vile master. They were to do this, not because they were compelled by force, but by their own free choice. As God's free men, they could choose for God's sake to be subject to every human institution. They had received grace from Christ for this very thing. They were not to use their freedom as a pretext for lawlessness.

Lawlessness is hateful to God, and the church should never embrace it. The welfare of the kingdom of God is best served by good order. The church itself has a vested interest in maintaining public stability and peace. It cannot properly fulfil its mandate (to preach, teach, and to nurture the souls of men) in conditions of social disruption and disorder. Anarchy and confusion are inimical to the mission of the church. A church that engages in revolution is against itself.[27]

It can be seen then that God is the source of all authority in the universe. All who act in a function appointed by God - in government, law, school, church, home - act in the strength of his delegated authority. They may not recognise God as the source of their authority, but **we are instructed to recognise it and ordinarily to yield to it.**

In the two passages quoted, there are two basic commands: the positive one, to be submissive to delegated authority as to God

[27] I am speaking for the church as an organized entity. It is not difficult to imagine situations where individual Christians might feel obliged to take up arms against injustice, tyranny, or crime, locally and internationally. After all, Christians may by numbered among those "magistrates who bear the sword" Ro 14:4, and they carry it nor for decoration but for destruction. But the **church** needs a peaceful and ordered society for the effective fulfillment of its mission; it has no business wielding weapons of death or fomenting revolutions

himself; and the negative one, **do not resist authority, for to do so is to resist God.**

Are there no exceptions to these rules?

There is in fact one strong exception: no authority should be obeyed when it is acting without authority!

For example: no Christian is obliged by God to obey a government that forbids him to worship God, or commands him to steal, or to act in any way against the laws of God. God has given no ruler authority to violate his laws or to interfere in the free worship of his people. Governments that attempt to do such things should be disobeyed. A church that permits government control over its beliefs and ministry is wishing death to itself as surely as one that encourages the destruction of law and order.

The great principle that motivated the apostle is clear: the church was to follow a policy that best reflected the authority of God, and that best enabled it to fulfil its evangelical mandate.

Ordinarily the outworking of that principle requires the church to be subject to whatever government and laws are currently functioning. In rare and extreme circumstances the same principle may require the church to endorse either passive disobedience, or even active resistance.

Under most circumstances, and particularly where the actions of any given authority do not violate a specific command of God, Christians should accept submission as the proper rule.

Paul breaks this rule into four symbols (Ro 13:7) -

> "Pay all of them their dues
> taxes to whom taxes are due
> revenue to whom revenue is due
> respect to whom respect is due
> honour to whom honour is due."

Those four symbols embrace authority in all of its expressions, levels, and forms. Let each Christian humbly use what authority God has given him; let each Christian humbly submit to what authority God has placed over him. Let all heed the admonition Paul adds to his remarks about our place in society: "Owe no one anything, except to love one another; for he who loves his neighbour has fulfilled the law... Love does no wrong to a neighbour" (vs. 8-10).

Peter's final admonition in the same context is similar: "Clothe yourselves, all of you, with humility toward one another, for 'God opposes the proud, but gives grace to the humble.' Humble yourselves therefore under the mighty hand of God, that in due time he may exalt you" (1 Pe 5:5-6).

The exhortation here is not to "feel" humble, nor to pray for humility, but to act with humility. It is not something to ask God for, it is something to do.

The strength of the expression "clothe yourselves with humility" is shown by a remarkable use some early Christians made of it. In Greek it is linked with a long apron slaves used to put on when they were doing servile work. Some early Christians were so moved by this idea that they deliberately sold themselves into slavery so that they might better witness to those who were in bondage! They understood that human pride of office is utterly irrelevant to the kingdom of God. They understood that God needs witnesses at every level of human society, and that it is as honourable to serve God at the side of a slave as to serve him at the side of an emperor.

Some of his servants God elevates to high places, for he has work for them there; others he hides in obscurity, for he has work for them there. We serve him well when we serve him where he has placed us.

Who does God oppose? The proud.

To whom does he give grace?  The humble.

Thus Peter confirmed when he quoted the words of Proverbs 3:34...

> *"God opposes the proud, but gives grace to the humble" (1 Pe 5:5).*

# CHAPTER EIGHT

# FOUR WAYS TO WALK

What does God require of you in your daily relationship with him? How should you structure your devotional life? What behaviour pattern is the most Christ-like?

For that matter, how did Jesus himself live day by day? How often did he pray? How much time did he spend reading scripture? What kind of things did he pray about? What life-style did he follow?

Is there one devotional pattern which is more Christ-like than any other?

There is surprising variety in the ways Christians have chosen to answer these questions; and this variety has led to life-styles that are astonishingly diverse from each other. At times one devotional pattern has been predominant, at times another. Most of them still survive today.

I have tried to analyse these various patterns, and to reduce them to certain common elements, and I have concluded from this analysis that there are **four basic styles** of Christian life: **Pragmatism, Pietism, Illuminism,** and **Passivism.**

If you do much reading in philosophy or church history you will come across all four of those terms, but they will not have quite the same meaning as I am giving them here. In philosophy and church history they are used in a limited technical sense: they describe specific groups of people, or ideas, that have flourished from time to time.

But in this Chapter I have adopted them as general descriptions of four kinds of Christian devotional behaviour. Here they mean only what I intend them to mean. So if you happen to be familiar with the technical and historical use of these four words, I must ask you to put those meanings aside for the moment and to accept the definitions I am giving them here.

I am suggesting, then, that there are four general patterns Christians follow as they attempt to structure their lives in a way that they believe will please God. Each of these patterns is a valid expression of Christian life. They each reflect some aspects of the model of godliness presented in scripture. They each have their strengths and weaknesses.

Later in this Chapter I will attempt a synthesis of these patterns; but just now let us look at them one by one. You will realise that there is a certain logic in the order in which I have placed them; but this should not be taken as an indication of their relative importance. The order is one of fitness, not of value.[28]

## PRAGMATISM

1. The pragmatist seeks to structure Christian life largely on a basis of informed reason, linked with responsible self-discipline and stewardship.

He believes that Christian life should be approached on a rational rather than an emotional basis, so he tends to be repulsed by overt

[28] As I have already mentioned, in the paragraphs that follow (and indeed throughout all of your lessons), wherever it is appropriate to do so please include the feminine gender in the masculine and vice versa. (see my note added to the table of contents above.)

emotionalism in religion and worship. His emphasis is on mind and will, rather than on heart and feeling.

2. He is deeply devoted to God, and is as willing to suffer for Christ, and to lose his life for the church, as any other Christian might be; but he dislikes public displays of piety, and he has little patience with those who parade their faith before the world.

Hence he does not feel obliged to say grace aloud in a restaurant, or to wear lapel buttons, or to put stickers on his car, or to hang texts on his wall, or in any way to display his piety in public uninvited. He thinks such overt behaviour verges on fanaticism, is rather crass, certainly rude, and tends to cheapen the gospel.

3. He is irritated by Christians whose religious experience seems to be encompassed in only three things: a small set of rigid doctrines; personal emotional experience; and a fixed pattern of devotional behaviour. He tends to equate such "fundamentalism" with bigotry, and to think that it ill reflects the true spirit of Christ.

Such narrow piety seems to him to be a self-centred form of Christianity, and one that is false to the real nature of the gospel. He demands a system that compels doctrine to spill over into the real world, and to become involved in the "non-spiritual" needs of people.

He reckons that many "pious" Christians, who claim to have answers to every problem, are simply demonstrating their lack of awareness. He thinks they have become so insulated from real life that they just don't see the problems and hurts their neighbours are experiencing. If they were more truly aware of the problems (says the pragmatist) these pious Christians would not be so sure of their answers. In fact, he thinks they are probably careful to avoid encountering many of the desperate problems society faces, lest their pat answers be probed too deeply.

But just as he is suspicious of pietistic easy answers to social and community problems, the pragmatist also rejects instant answers to personal and spiritual problems. Thus -

4. He will not accept doctrines that pretend to provide immediate sanctification, or perfect victory over sin, or a final solution to any of life's pressing dilemmas.

He is much more inclined to a scenario that portrays the Christian as growing steadily in maturity, righteousness, and strength, through many struggles and constant learning.

He thinks it is a delusion, a distortion of scripture, to teach that there is a one-stop solution to any of the major conflicts that confront people from day to day.

5. He is sceptical about the claims of some pietists that the Bible is their only authority; for it is obvious to him that, in practice, the real authority for such people is not scripture alone, but scripture as interpreted by the church - or worse, as interpreted by a single leader in the church.

He sees a censorship that he thinks is scandalous operating in these groups. The people are tightly controlled in the doctrines they are permitted to believe, the books they are permitted to read, the Bible teachers they are permitted to encounter, the recreations and culture they are permitted to follow, and so on.

That approach to Christianity is anathema to him. He believes it produces spiritual juveniles, not mature sons of God. The real authority over those people is not biblical (says the pragmatist) but ecclesiastical. He utterly rejects that kind of censorship over his mind or spirit, and he reserves the right to allow scripture to speak to him in any way that is good for him.

6. He believes firmly in Paul's injunction, "Prove all things;" hence he may be addicted to what he is pleased to call "intellectual honesty" - although in his pursuit of objective truth he may be

willing to bend scripture to conform to ideas that are currently popular in the secular world.

He is in fact happy to use all of the tools and resources of modern society as he seeks to formulate a Christian way of life. Hence he is willing to accept the insights of philosophy, sociology, psychology, science, etc, and he may tend to adapt the gospel to suit these insights rather than adapt these insights to suit the gospel.

He tends to want academic respectability, or to seek the approval of secular scholarship, and he dislikes a doctrinaire approach to the Bible.

His ideals may be as high, and his doctrines as firmly believed, as those of the most starry-eyed pietist; but he is much more willing to adopt practical compromises. Thus he is flexible in his approach to doctrine and life, to ideals and situations. A situational approach to ethics is more likely to appeal to him than a dogmatic or casuistic approach.

7. He is willing to allow respect for the views of other people.

He may be satisfied that his own beliefs are true and reliable, but he is not inclined to adopt an exclusivist attitude. So he readily acknowledges the merits of views other than his own, and is just as frank about the weaknesses inherent in his own views.

He is not afraid of doubt, but is willing to ask any questions that need to be asked, and to follow the answers wherever they may lead.

Yet that very tendency to ask questions rather than provide answers can bring him under Paul's indictment, as one of those "who will listen to anybody but can never arrive at a knowledge of the truth" (2 Ti 3:7).

8. He tends to be suspicious of anything that claims to be supernatural, and he will offer a rational explanation for many supposed miracles.

This scepticism sometimes extends even to the biblical miracles, and devastates faith. Scepticism rather than credulity is, in fact, both the virtue and the vice of pragmatism. Even when a pragmatist accepts the supernatural in theory he often dispenses with it in practice. He has little expectation that a miracle either can or will occur in his time.

He tends to emphasise divine transcendence, and prefers God at a distance; he is rather uncomfortable with an imminent deity. Not that he does not love God. He does. But he prefers to work out his own salvation, even with fear and trembling, rather than to have God too close at hand working it out for him.

9. He tends to ignore, or even scorn, any kind of "inner illumination", and places little or no value on "dreams", "visions", "voices", and the like.

He is suspicious of anything that is not subject to rational analysis, and he is quick to point out that visions, dreams, inner voices, and the like, are not uniquely Christian, but are equally common in pagan practice.

He is especially suspicious of any "guidance" that is presumed to have a supernatural origin. He doubts that God interferes often in the lives of Christian people. He believes rather that the Lord leaves his people free to serve him in the way which seems best to each one of them.

He has a flexible view of the will of God. He is not inclined to believe that God has a fixed purpose for every Christian, but believes that for most Christians the purpose of God is fully expressed in such scriptures as 1 Th 4:1-8; Tit 2:11-14; etc.

Within such a general framework of godly living, he thinks that each Christian is free to determine his own way of life, to choose his own spouse, home, career, recreation, etc.

However, the pragmatist allows that there are certainly some individuals whose lives are specifically directed by God, as were the lives of Abraham, Moses, David, Paul, Luther, Wesley, and so on.

10. He tends to feel that God is better served through sanctified common sense, and through mature decisions based on responsible thought, than through unplanned actions based on some inner revelation. So he prefers a reasoned approach to life and faith, and depends a great deal on wisdom and maturity wrought by wide experience.

He believes he should relate to God, not as an infant needing to be led by the hand, but as an intelligent, responsible, and adult son. He cannot understand Christians who seem to him to develop a puppet-on-a-string response to God, void of personal choice and responsibility.

He thinks that God mostly leaves him free to make his own decisions, even when they are wrong. He is impatient with "pious" Christians who refuse to accept responsibility for making decisions, but try to make God responsible for everything.

He believes there are no easy answers, either in life or in scripture, and that many decisions can be made, and conflicts resolved, only after much mental and spiritual travail.

11. For that reason, he fully accepts the blame for his mistakes, and he is happy to accept credit for his successes, without neglecting to give thanks to God. He thinks that Christians who make a show of accepting no praise for their achievements, but lash themselves when they fail, are behaving unnaturally, and are probably hypocrites.

He claims that Christians who depend on divine guidance in every matter, and who are perpetually seeking "the leading of the Spirit" make God as fickle and changeable as they are themselves. It seems to him that these people maintain their stance on guidance only by much self-delusion, or by developing short memories - they have a marvellous ability to evade the embarrassment of God seeming to contradict today what he said to them yesterday.

The pragmatist attitude (he says) at least allows him to keep all of his options open. He may change his mind today about a decision he made yesterday without being obliged to make God responsible for the change.

12. He allows the use in worship of virtually any object, custom, liturgy, art form, or expression that can be seen to have aesthetic, cultural, or religious value.

In the same way, he usually allows liberty in the observance of personal and cultural mores, and scorns those who try to build righteousness around a host of taboos.

He claims that many actions are of indifferent moral value because they are neither commanded nor condemned by God. So he allows himself a personal freedom and indulgence that often seems scandalous to some more pious souls.

The conscience of a pragmatist tends to be quite pragmatic. He refuses to make a sharp distinction between "secular" and "sacred", "worldly" and "spiritual", and believes that almost anything that scripture does not specifically condemn may be used with thanksgiving and for the glory of God.

13. He is proud of his cultural and social freedom and tends to pity those whose more restricted ideas of worldliness, and whose distinctions between secular and sacred, isolate them (as he sees it) from many pleasures and recreations.

In his disposition towards naturalism in his life-style (rather than supernaturalism), he abhors the use of religious jargon, and he tries to use ordinary speech forms both inside and outside the church. He endeavours to be natural, relaxed, and easy in his Christian walk. He does not have a heightened sense of sin, and he likes to think he is free of "religious hang-ups".

But for those same reasons, he may allow worship to become formal and ceremonial to the point of destroying spiritual freedom and vitality. Worship for him may thus become a spectacle rather than an act of communal fellowship and participation.

14. Because of his tendency to adopt a devitalising relativism in his approach to scripture, the pragmatist may become lax in his ethical and moral standards. He may also tend toward an undue conformity to the ideas and ways of the world until he becomes outwardly indistinguishable from an unbeliever.

He may come to have more faith in the power of social and political action to change society than in the power of proclaiming the gospel. He may easily become a kind of modern Sadducee.

But if the pragmatist at his worst is the modern equivalent of a Sadducee, then the next category, the pietist, at his worst is a contemporary Pharisee ...

## PIETISM

Extreme pragmatists and extreme pietists represent opposite ends of the Christian spectrum.

As I have suggested, in their worst forms they are the modern equivalents of the ancient Sadducees and Pharisees who were so abhorred by Jesus. But conversely, in their best forms both of these devotional patterns represent valid and necessary expressions of the Christian faith.

Not all who are disposed toward a pragmatic approach would embrace all of the aspects I have listed above, any more than all who may fall into a pietistic category would embrace all of the points I have listed below. Any such list cannot avoid being to some extent a caricature. But I think that the major emphases, or trends, of each category are fairly well defined, and you will probably find yourself relating more closely to one than to the other.

1. A pietist is characterised by deep and evident love for God, scripture, and the church, and by a desire to express that love in every part of his life.

He cannot hide his Christianity from the world. On the contrary, he is far more prone to adopt a life style that will leave the world in no doubt at all that he is a Christian. He cannot conceive of a Christianity which is not visible, separated, aggressive, and even abrasive.

Without him the church would have lost its heartbeat of evangelism; the cause of Christ would have been reduced to an intellectual exercise in religious philosophy. The gospel mandate would have become a program of social reform, instead of a burning mission to rescue men and women from endless death.

2. He is motivated by a desire for holiness that must be expressed in daily life; he cannot accept holiness as something heavenly, invisible, intangible, not felt nor seen. To him, if holiness does not exist in life, then it does not exist at all.

He understands holiness as something that is experienced by the believer and is then translated into a visible and God-centred life-style.

Like Paul, he thinks with sorrow of those who claim to be Christian, yet their God seems to be their belly, and their minds are fixed on earthly things more than heavenly (Ph 3:18-19).

He cannot conceive of any Christian living comfortably in this world - for are we not called to take up our cross and to follow Christ? Did not the Lord say that friendship with the world is enmity with God, and that in the world we would have tribulation?

3. He seeks to develop a life-style that elevates the spiritual dimension of human nature above the mind and the body. He sees this as man's true calling, and that any form of earth-centred life-style simply denies man's true nature and reduces him to animal level.

To inculcate this spiritual life-style, he delights in prayer, in the devotional study of scripture, in worship, in praise, and in anything that might enhance his active fellowship with God. He would rather be in the Lord's house, in prayer, than anywhere else in the world.

Without him, prayer would long since have vanished from the church, or it would have become a thing of meaningless routine.

The pragmatist is often too busy to pray, or may have little confidence in its efficacy. He may depend more on human effort and skill. But the pietist believes that prayer is the only source of spiritual power, and that nothing worthwhile can be achieved by the church apart from fervent and effectual prayer.

His example has kept the whole church aware of the immense spiritual resource God has given to us in prayer.

His separated life, his call for holiness, has also kept the church from being overwhelmed by secularity; he has forced the church to retain its distinct identity and to remain a thorn in the world's flesh.

4. But this demand for a visible expression of "holiness", when it is placed beside the claim to be "spiritual", often creates for the pietist a state of tension in which he tends to veer from doing nothing to prove he is "spiritual", to doing too much to prove he is "holy".

Also, his very love for the church, his very sense of the high calling of worship, his total involvement with the life of faith, may lead him to neglect other matters of social and community concern that are equally emphasised in scripture.

His desire for a truly "spiritual" identity, linked with his passion for a visible form of "holiness" may lead him to structure his Christian life largely around overt acts of devotion, such as set times of daily prayer, a fixed pattern of Bible reading, etc. He tends to make rules of such things, and to feel righteous if he keeps his rules, but unrighteous if he neglects them.

5. The pietist is aiming to achieve a state of genuine godliness; but a pragmatist might accuse him of mere outward conformity to his own presuppositions about what is, or is not, "spiritual".

For example: a vicar once told me a story about learning humility in a Christian community. He came down to breakfast intending to read a newspaper while he ate; but he saw another man reading a Bible. The vicar, with a blush of shame, discarded the paper, and read his Bible instead! In telling this story, the vicar never imagined that his response could be challenged. Surely it is more "spiritual", more "righteous", to read the Bible than a newspaper?

A pietist will usually assume that "spiritual" activities are preferable to those that are "mundane". He sees a distinction between secular and sacred that a pragmatist would never allow.

A pragmatist would retort that sometimes it is just as godly to read a newspaper as a Bible. He would ask why the Bible-reader, out of love and respect for the vicar, did not hastily put aside his Bible and read a paper instead?

The pragmatist would suspect that the pious Bible-reader (like a true Pharisee) probably rustled the pages of his Bible more loudly in an effort to provoke the paper-reader into a "holy" activity!

Pietists and pragmatists are not usually very comfortable with each other.

6. He tends to be ethically rigorous, and to reflect the sharp distinctions between sin and righteousness that are apparent in scripture. He desires to emulate his Lord by loving righteousness and hating iniquity.

He has a horror of becoming "worldly", and he heartily endorses the sentiments of 1 Jn 2:15-17. Texts like that are among his favourite scriptures.

But for that reason he has a tendency to descend to a Pharisaical practice of certain social mores and taboos, which are far more cultural than scriptural in origin.

Thus he is prone to equate holiness with the observance of certain group strictures on matters of dress, entertainment, personal habits, diet, drinking, recreation, literature, art, music, etc.

By contrast, a pragmatist would argue that such things have almost nothing to do with holiness, which he reckons to be a thing of the spirit, not of mere outward behaviour, nor of mere conformity to a set of taboos.

7. He tends toward an ascetic pattern of behaviour, based on his belief that the flesh must be denied if the spirit is to triumph.

He is opposed to anything that might be construed as mere self-indulgence.

There is, of course, much scripture to support this approach, and the pietist argues properly for a separated, self-denying life-style. Yet this may tend toward an improper abhorrence of the physical side of life, and in particular to a "guilt complex" about the enjoyment of sensual pleasures. His asceticism may become far more self-centred than God-centred.

In fact, his constant endeavours toward holiness, separation, and victory over sin, always risk drawing him into an unhappy self-centredness. In this state he thinks constantly about himself, and is ever more deeply engrossed with his own needs and problems, to the neglect of his wider responsibilities.

A pragmatist, by contrast, tends to be far more concerned with the needs of the world around him, or with the larger needs of the church, and he is hardly interested at all in polishing himself to spiritual perfection.

8. As a mark of his separation from the world, and perhaps also of his anxiety about its power to entice him away from Christ, he has a tendency to despise intellectual and cultural development, and to withdraw from involvement in social, political, or civic affairs.

He argues that the church can be "the salt of the earth" only if it keeps its "savour" through a practice of strict separation.

But the pragmatist would say (as he reaches toward public office and social reform) that salt savours nothing until it becomes deeply involved with the thing it is savouring.

9. He has a fervent love for scripture, and views it absolutely as the inspired, and completely supernatural word of God. He believes that God speaks to him through scripture, and desires to search it continuously, looking for divine revelation, and seeking principles on which he may build his life.

This makes him a ready exponent of scripture, a man of penetrating spiritual insight. His faith is sure, being grounded in the promise of God. He has a close relationship with God, a confidence in believing, an experience of answered prayer, that a pragmatist may never know.

Because of him the church has remained a supernatural body, infused by the Holy Spirit; whereas it may well have become an entirely natural organisation, lacking any divine resource.

Generally speaking, pietists have an expectation of miracles that pragmatists lack.

10. But this vital sense of the voice of God in scripture, this awe of its supernatural character, this deep love for the sacred pages, may lead the pietist to an unfounded proof-texting, and to a kind of superstitious bibliolatry as he hunts the pages of his Bible, or stabs his finger blindly, for "a word from God".

Even when a pragmatist and a pietist are equally committed to the authority and inerrancy of the Bible, they tend to approach it differently. The pragmatist with his more this-worldly approach tends to be bemused by the supernaturalism of the pietist with his more other-worldly approach.

For example, consider Ps 119:11 - "I have laid up thy word in my heart that I might not sin against thee." A pietist would tend to see in that verse a claim that the word of God possesses supernatural power to drive sin away from those who plant that word in their hearts. A pragmatist would be inclined to read it simply as an instruction to memorise the commandments so that he did not unwittingly break one of God's laws.

In general, the pragmatist is inclined to give the Bible its plain, unadorned surface meaning, and to read it like he would any other book. But the pietist, because he invests scripture with a special kind of supernatural aura, is inclined to read the Bible in a special way, and to search for its "deeper", more "spiritual" meaning.

11. The pietist has a keen awareness of sin, and an unfailing desire for purity; thus he tends to be introspective and continually uneasy about himself. Indeed he may never achieve a harmonious and pleasant relationship with himself or with God.

The pragmatist pities this perpetual inner disturbance; but the pietist argues that his life-style is nearer to scripture than the other, while citing perhaps Ga 5:16-17.

If he ever began to feel easy about himself, or placid about his spiritual life, he would at once be anxious lest his conscience had become dulled. He would be apprehensive about Satan lulling him into a false security so that he was no longer advancing spiritually. He is more aware than the pragmatist of the activity of Satan.

12. But in all of this the pietist has a weakness. Despite his inbuilt resistance against reaching a place of inner spiritual rest, despite his instinct to dig up new sins of which to accuse himself, he never stops searching for some key to "perfection", a final solution to the problem of "holiness".

So he provides a good market for writers of devotional books who offer an easy way to personal victory, a single answer to entire sanctification, or a simple pattern for discovering and doing the will of God (the "higher-deeper-surrendered-crucified-overcoming life" syndrome). None of these books has ever solved his problems, but he is always ready for the next one.

Thus his spiritual hunger drives him to continue his search; but his concept of righteousness precludes him from reaching his goal.

13. He is attracted to scriptures that speak about "dying to self", and likes the idea of becoming nothing so that God might be everything, and of being fully emptied of "self" in order to become full of God, and so on.

An example: a pietist, preaching on the story of Gideon, fastened at once on the idea, "God cannot use me until I become nothing." He declared that the key verse in the story is Jg 6:15, "Pray, Lord, how can I deliver Israel? Behold, my clan is the weakest in Manasseh, and I am the least in my family." The pietist claimed that this humble confession was the basis of all of Gideon's subsequent triumphs, and that we likewise must become "nothing" before God can use us.

But a pragmatist who was present protested that he saw the text quite differently. To him, Gideon deserved to be censured, not commended, for that wretched and defeatist confession. He insisted that the emphasis should rather be placed on the Lord's demand that Gideon should rise up in all the strength of his manhood and do exploits for God and Israel! (vs.14)

In that same sermon, the pietist quoted Jn 12:24, "Unless a grain of wheat falls into the earth and dies, it remains alone; but if it dies, it bears much fruit." He said, "This passage confirms that Gideon had to 'die', to become nothing, to forsake all of his own abilities, to depend on nothing in himself, before he could serve God." But the pragmatist retorted that **he** would apply Jesus' words only to Gideon's need to crucify his timidity, his negative thinking, and his reluctance to obey God, so that he could then march out with faith and valour, using all of his skill to deliver and rule Israel.

14. The pietist is prone to feel that his is the only truly valid form of Christianity, and that other forms (especially the pragmatic) are at best inferior and at worst altogether non-Christian.

He finds firm spiritual security in his identification with a group that is clearly definable at a local and worldwide level. He knows that he belongs to a brotherhood that has a similar cultural and religious expression around the world.

He majors on knowledge, not on doubt. His favourite expression is, "I know." He believes he is equal to any situation. But his confidence may be artificial; for he may "know" only because he has not allowed himself to face questions he cannot answer; and he may be strong only because he has not allowed himself to encounter situations where he would be weak.

A pragmatist is more prone to ask questions, and to confess the weaknesses and infirmities he shares with his ungodly neighbours.

15. The pietist has confidence in his doctrines. He trusts in the ability they give him to cope with any situation. He rejoices in his group identity. These things draw him toward an overt display of his

religious beliefs, in both speech and conduct, and to a religious practice based on conformity to group behaviour.

That in turn leads him also to the use of certain standard words, expressions, or patterns of speech (a kind of professional Christian jargon), which then clearly identify him as an initiated member of the group.

As a further expression of this sense of "belonging", and of the intensely personal nature of this kind of Christian experience, pietistic songs and worship may often be more concerned with personal blessing ("Oh! That will be glory for me!") than with offering praise to the majesty and glory of God.

16. He is very sensitive to the voice of God, and is concerned primarily to discover the will of God and to do it.

He is inclined to believe that God has a particular plan for his life, a divine purpose that embraces every aspect of life, and that he can truly prosper only as he aligns himself with this plan.

He seeks to discover the divine purpose through scripture, and through the counsel of mature friends; but most of all, he expects God to speak to him inwardly, in response to prayer. He understands the spiritual significance of Is 30:20-21.

But this dependence on direct and specific guidance, even in small matters, makes him susceptible to misdirection. He may misconstrue mere whim and emotional prompting, or worse, his own secret wishes, as the voice of God.

He is given to expressions (which pragmatists find most irritating) such as, "the Lord told me to do this," "the Lord said I should buy this," "God told me to say it."

Pragmatists are inclined to think that such "guidance" comes more likely from a perfervid imagination than from the Holy Spirit.

17. The pietist is persuaded that only what is done for God in faith, born out of prayer, and guided by the Holy Spirit, has any spiritual value. What is done in "the flesh", motivated by self-will, a product of mere human planning and skill, is carnal and unprofitable.

While he does use natural means and skills, he seeks at all times to be undergirded by a divine and supernatural enabling. All that he does, he wants to do in the ability God gives. He is profoundly committed to a supernaturalism that expects direct and immediate divine intervention in every situation.

He seeks a conscious sense of God's presence, and is unhappy if it is lacking. This supernaturalism, this sense of the divine, makes him wary of intellectualism, and leaves him open to emotionalism. He may be suspicious both of too much formality in worship, and of too much scholarship. He is inclined to think that in the end academic attainment is worth very little in contrast with spiritual development.

Thus feelings are prone to be more important to him than knowledge, experience more significant than doctrine.

## AN INTERIM COMMENT

If I have succeeded in my task, and have not allowed my own bias to become too apparent, you should now be aware that pragmatists and pietists both have many virtues and many faults. Both groups have been with the church from the beginning, and will be with it to the end. The church needs them both.

Pragmatists have been a source of stability, unity, continuity, scholarship, sound doctrine, and sound administration. But if the church had only had pragmatists it would long since have frozen into cold and sterile formality.

Pietists have been a source of fiery zeal, of missionary endeavour; they have fostered a desire for holy living and the authority of scripture; they have kept emotion alive in worship; and they have produced most of the hymns, songs, and choruses sung by Christians around the world. But if the church had only had pietists it would long since have either disintegrated into fanaticism, discord, and individualism, or it would have fallen under the despotic sway of spiritual dictators.

Where either the pragmatic or pietistic influence has been denied its rightful place, harm has invariably followed. Hence churches can be found, intellectual, stiff, formal, having a show of godliness, but denying all the power of it. The apostle said that he would have nothing to do with such a church (2 Ti 3:5).

Other churches can be found, legalistic, conformist, autocratic, dominated by rules and by the personalities of leaders. And there are pietistic splinter groups, fanatical about minutiae of doctrine or of behaviour, fiercely independent, wild and unruly, acknowledging no law but their own.

All of them have removed themselves from the wisdom of God. A better path would be to avoid both pragmatic and pietistic follies, and strive to embrace the virtues of each.

(This study of life-styles is continued in the next Chapter.)

# CHAPTER NINE

# A MORE ABUNDANT LIFE

In the previous Chapter we began to explore the four kinds of life-styles that Christians across the centuries have adopted. Out of those four, the two that we have already considered - **pragmatism** and **pietism** - embrace most Christians. The remaining two categories **(illuminism** and **passivism)** are really branches of pietism; but they are distinct enough to justify separate treatment -

## ILLUMINISM AND PASSIVISM

It is difficult for me to write objectively about illuminism and passivism, because they seem to me more like Christian aberrations than valid expressions of the faith. Yet though to my eye they appear to be exaggerated if not distorted life-styles, I am bound to acknowledge that many godly people have found in these categories the best way to express their relationship with God.

I also freely acknowledge that the church has been enriched in many ways by its illuminists and passivists. Without them we would all be very much poorer.

Here then is a comment, I hope not too much biased, on what it means to be an illuminist, or a passivist.

### Illuminism

1. An illuminist is a Christian who earnestly desires to live in constant and immediate contact with God. He strives to develop a

sensitivity to the Holy Spirit that will enable him to respond instantly to the most gentle divine promptings.

He believes that God is directly involved in every part of Christian life, and that he should seek spiritual guidance in even the most trivial matters. He would not, of course, allow the adjective "trivial". He believes rather that every event in his life, even the seemingly unimportant, may be fraught with eternal significance.

He sees the hand of God in every happening. He looks for the working of God in every incident. Nothing that happens to him is meaningless.

2. He believes implicitly that, since God has a purpose to fulfil in every event, it is imperative to obtain divine guidance before doing anything. He is reluctant to make his own decisions or to act on his own authority in any matter at all.

He will not allow that he is personally responsible for the daily pattern of life, but seeks a mandate from heaven before engaging in even the most trifling and mundane activities (although, once again, he would again protest against my adjectives).

3. He expects guidance to come from God directly and personally, not indirectly nor impersonally.

By contrast, pragmatists and moderate pietists may seek direct guidance only rarely; in the main, they simply accept as a matter of faith that God is in control of their lives, ordering things according to his will.

But that is not sufficient for an illuminist. He craves a far more personal involvement with the divine. He wants to hear the voice of God, to see the face of God, to know, tangibly, experientially, that he is being guided by God.

So he is not content to receive guidance always indirectly, from circumstances, or from the church, or even from the Bible. He wants his knowledge of God's will to come immediately and personally from God himself.

That is why he is called an "illuminist": because by a "voice", a "vision", or some other act of divine intervention, he is seeking an inner "illumination" that will give him unfailing knowledge of God's will in every situation.

4. Because of his reliance on immediate guidance by God, an illuminist may seem to other Christians to be given to irrational and erratic conduct. But the illuminist offers what to him is always sufficient justification for his actions: "The Lord told me ... led me ... showed me ... I must obey God rather than man."

Such a claim is very hard to argue against, and it greatly exasperates other Christians, who may feel that God is being blamed for some quite misguided and foolish actions. But when an illuminist claims God himself as the authority for his actions, there is no higher authority his opponents can claim against him.

To an illuminist neither church nor scripture can speak with greater authority than God. Illuminists, therefore, are disliked by pragmatists, who tend to enforce conformity to order, and also by pietists, who tend to enforce conformity to authority.

But the illuminist refuses to be bound by either order or authority. He is resolved to submit to the voice of God alone.

5. He is greatly inclined to stress individual liberty; indeed, without him freedom of conscience may well have been destroyed in the church. He and his brothers have had an immense and beneficial influence on the religious and political life of our community.

Christian mysticism (another name for illuminism) has profoundly affected the development of our democratic institutions and of the religious liberties we enjoy. Illuminist movements, such as the Society of Friends (Quakers), have exercised an influence far greater than their size would indicate.

To these people nothing has been more important than "the inner light" and the freedom to walk in that light. For this liberty they have argued and evangelised, and even laid down their lives. Furthermore, through their insistence on the right of women, as well as men, to have access to this "light", they have had a notable influence on the high status women enjoy in our society.

They have also been among the strongest proponents in the church for the priesthood of every believer, tirelessly advocating the right of every Christian to bypass every authority, ecclesiastical and political, and to go straight into God's presence.

Their struggles against arbitrary authority and for freedom of conscience have greatly enhanced the religious and political liberties that are now an accepted part of our democratic way of life.

6. Illuminists may be described as having three main characteristics: (a) an intense awareness of God, marked by deep confession of sin and unceasing prayer; (b) a life lived under the direct and total control of God; and (c) a very personal, highly cultivated, experience of God.

The illuminist's special value to the church lies in his promotion of this individualistic and personal relationship with God, and in the rich legacy of devotional literature, prayers, poems, and hymns, he has given to the church.

So long as he remains, it will not be possible for a sterile formality nor a dogmatic autocracy to overwhelm the spiritual life of the people. He prevents both ceremony and dogma from being exalted at the expense of experience and practice.

But his life-style also has in it the seeds of heresy: that is, of ignoring biblical norms and sound doctrine; of concentrating on personal salvation to the exclusion of wider expressions of Christian concern and compassion; of developing a simplistic faith that scorns scholarship; of belittling any knowledge of God or of scripture that is gained through ordinary processes of diligent study; of exalting "knowledge" gained by "revelation", or by some experience of inner "illumination", above reason and scripture; and of an unstable and erratic emotionalism that destroys genuine spiritual growth and maturity.

## Passivism

A better name for this life-style may have been "quietism"; but I finally chose passivism, because quietism is too closely linked with specific groups and movements in the history of the church. "Passivism" gives a broader scope to the life-style I am discussing here.

Both names, however, may be said to describe "a form of religious mysticism requiring abandonment of the will, withdrawal from worldly interests, and passive meditation on God and divine things" (World Book Dictionary).

1.  A passivist seeks to be totally God-centred. To achieve the goal of being consumed by the divine, he is willing to deny all self-identity and to abnegate utterly the flesh, so that the spirit may reign supreme. He believes that his spiritual life cannot flourish until his physical life is all but eradicated. If it were possible to do so without suicide, he would prefer to cease physical activity altogether.

2.  He seeks a profound love-relationship with God, and believes that the human soul's noblest occupation is an all-engrossing contemplation of heaven. His fervent aspiration is to see God face to face, to see him as he actually is - sometimes called the Beatific Vision.

By the pathway of being totally absorbed with God, he seeks to anticipate the bliss, the exalted happiness, that will be given to all of the righteous when they enter heaven. But he is not content to wait until death, nor for the day of resurrection; he desires an open vision of God now, in this life, and believes that he can obtain it.

3.  To attain that openness of spiritual vision, he is willing to renounce his intellect, will, and emotions. No feeling, no personal ambition, no learning - nothing at all - can be allowed to intrude upon his relationship with God. His overwhelming desire is to achieve unsullied union with the divine, to lose his soul, even his personal awareness, in the boundlessness of heaven's glory.

That quest may draw him to the practice of extreme asceticism, even to self-flagellation and the infliction of various other kinds of physical torment. At the least, it will probably drive him to deprive himself of many ordinary comforts, perhaps even many necessities.

No merely personal desire can be tolerated. The flesh, the ego, must be thoroughly subdued. Even the slightest degree of pride of accomplishment, of self satisfaction, or of personal gratification, is obnoxious. Indeed, he seeks to remove as much as possible from both his mind and his speech all consciousness of self; for him, the most forbidden word is "I".

However, his greatest problem lies in the fact that the more strenuously he struggles to eradicate "self" the more deeply conscious of himself he becomes! There may be no more egocentric person than one who is concentrating exclusively on becoming theocentric. The more he seeks to become "lost" in God the more likely he is to find only himself occupying his field of vision!

4.  He can become so extreme in his renunciation of self that he disregards all thought of reward and punishment, of heaven and hell, of Christian duty and joy, of church and society. He is the stuff of which hermits are made. He seeks a form of "mystic death" that bears more resemblance to the ideas of eastern religions and philosophies than it does to the gospel of Christ.

5.  In his quest for an abiding sense of God's presence he may lapse into a subjectivism in which inner feelings become the sole

arbiters of spiritual status. Faith may be reduced to nothing more than emotional sensation.

As a consequence, he tends to develop a love-relationship with God that to other Christians seems quite maudlin. In his poetry, hymns, and prayers he may use many expressions of endearment, a kind of love-language, which others would deem hardly appropriate to describe the creature's relationship with the Creator.

## SYNTHESIS

I have tried to be reasonably objective in my portrayal of those four Christian life-styles, and I hope my own preference (or should I say prejudice?) has remained discreetly unobtrusive. But in any case I have tried to expose the strengths as well as the weaknesses of each group as fairly as possible.

My purpose has been two-fold:

1. to show that, kept within proper limits, any one of those four categories can provide a framework within which a successful and God-honouring life can be built;

2. to show that each category, if pushed to an extreme, can lead to a distorted caricature of true Christian life.

My presentation of the categories has tended toward the caricatured rather than the moderate version. It should not be imagined, for example, that all Christians with a pragmatic disposition possess all of the characteristics I have listed; and the same is true of the other three. There are evidently many pragmatists who are half-way pietists, and pietists who are half-way pragmatists, and so on.

Nor do those four categories exhaust the possible ways in which people can structure their Christian lives, although they probably do cover the main or most commonly observed patterns. Most Christians could identify themselves in terms of one of them.

Now it should be salutary to realise that most of us will fall fairly readily into a certain category, and that the Christian life-style we reflect may not be the only or even the best way to be Christ-like. That realisation should make us cautious about criticising those whose style differs from ours.

There is not just one best way of Christian life that every believer should follow. The best way for you is the way that is best for you - that is, the way that is most harmonious with your own background, bias, and personality.

Hence we should refrain from claiming that other patterns of Christian life are somehow sub-Christian, and that the way you and I have chosen (or have been taught to follow) is the only valid method. What is valid for you, or for me, may be quite unconsonant for another.

In that respect pragmatists (by virtue of their very pragmatism) are inclined to be more tolerant than pietists (whose disposition is towards strictness). But we must all learn to accept each other lovingly, to recognise aspects of the multifaceted genius of God in each disparate life-style, and to acknowledge that the good health and prosperity of the church depends on each person being allowed to live as God intends him to live.

We can also learn from each other. I would think that a pragmatist who is fully open to the influence of the Holy Spirit, who is growing and maturing in Christ, would find himself becoming mellowed, modified, more fruitful, by the ingrafting of a generous measure of pietism. And the same should be true of a pietist. And pietists and pragmatists could both gain from a touch of illuminism and passivism!

Presumably, an ideal pattern might be to embrace the best elements of every category; but that is probably an unreal hope. Most of us will be strongly drawn to one life-style in preference to all others; and there is no harm in this, so long as we retain a charitable attitude toward those who differ from us.

This study will have served a good purpose if it makes people more aware of who they are, so that they more honestly appraise what they are doing. It is wise for you and me to acknowledge the limitations of our way of life, and to learn how to avoid extremes.

The best way to do that, and to rid ourselves of any kind of misanthropic exclusiveness, is to realise our own fallibility and to expose ourselves humbly and gladly to the ways and ideas of others.

Christ is the final example for us all - but I must allow that you may not see Christ just as I see him. To me, the Lord may reveal certain aspects of his richly diverse character; to you, he may show other facets, equally splendid, yet unique to your vision of the Saviour.

Thus to each of us there may be given a different image and view of the surpassing wonder and beauty of Jesus.

It will be enough for you and me if we each follow the Master in the way he chooses to reveal himself to us.

## LIVING ABUNDANTLY

"Few parts of scripture have been so violated in interpretation, from a psychological point of view, as Jesus' statement, 'Happy are the poor in spirit, for they shall see God.' Many Christians take that verse as a signal to cultivate a psychological 'poorness'. That 'such a worm as I' theology has become as useful to the masochistic Christian as the flagellation of the body with whips done in the Middle Ages."[29]

With those words Stanley Lindquist exposes a problem that is still real in the church: the problem of Christians who hate life, who seek a kind of spiritual immolation. Some of these people might actually dare to commit physical suicide if they could be sure it would be painless and was not forbidden by God!

They yearn to die and be with Christ - but only because they find no usefulness in this world. They hungrily turn to Bible passages that encourage their debilitating self-effacement - but they just as resolutely ignore contrary passages.

So (as Stanley Lindquist points out), "they take biblical teachings out of context, such as 'turn the other cheek,' 'never by angry,' 'put your brother before you' ... (Thus they gain) biblically backed reasons for doing nothing - for being **acted on instead of acting."**

Here then are two opposing ideas: to act; or to be acted on. Which of them reflects the pattern of scripture? Does God call us to a passive or to an active frame of mind?

Which is more Christian: to affirm life, or to **deny it?**

I want to offer my view that -

## 1. <u>God Does Not Want You To Deny Life</u>

There may well be exceptions to the ideas you will find in this Chapter, and it is certainly not my desire to pre-empt any divine prerogative. God is plainly free to call any of his children to follow any pattern he pleases. But apart from some special act of

---

[29] From an article, "How To Be Properly Poor," in Christianity Today, Sept, 12th 1975, pg 13. The Beatitude should read however , "... for theirs is the Kingdom of Heaven" (Mt 5:3)

divine providence, or some other extraordinary circumstance, I think scripture shows that the children of God are usually called to live positive, fulfilled, and active lives.

That is, you are called to affirm life, not to deny it; to act, not to be acted upon.

Many Christians, however, have chosen a different path: the way of self-inflicted privation. By harsh personal mortification, by renunciation of all so-called "worldly" pleasure, they have sought to be free of the trammels of "carnality", and thereby to discover a truly "Christ-like" way of life.

The hermits, flagellants, and mystics who have flourished at various times in the past provide a good example of this urge. They delighted in making life bitter. They lived in caves, mixed foul herbs and dust with their food, wore rough garments laced with thorns, put sharp stones in their shoes, slept on rocky beds, lacerated their own flesh with whips and knives, abstained from food, from speech, from human company, and from anything they deemed antagonistic to the spirit.

By such brutal disciplines they expected to crucify the flesh and to release the spirit into perfect communion with God. Many of them gained great fame as holy saints, and curious multitudes flocked to their dens and holes to gaze on them with awe.

Among the most extraordinary of the hermits were the stylites. These were ascetics who lived permanently on the top of a natural or artificial pillar (Gk. "stylos"), thus physically separating themselves from the world in order to seek pure fellowship with God. Some kind of shelter was usually built on top of the pillar, and food and other basic requirements were provided by admiring disciples.

## A) The Stylites

The most famous of the pillar-sitters is St. Simeon Stylites, who is the traditional founder of this form of religious life.[30] He lived c. 390-459 AD. When he was 30 years of age he was expelled from a strict monastery because his personal austerity was too extreme! He built a pillar six feet high and sat on it for ten years. Then he began to increase the height of the pillar from time to time until it finally stood sixty feet above the ground. He lived in stringent poverty on his platform at the top of the pillar for a total of thirty-six years, preaching to the crowds who stood gaping at its foot, and exercising an enormous influence!

The practice of that kind of asceticism has nearly vanished from the church; but the spirit of religious masochism it represents is still widespread, though in more subtle forms.

Nowadays people tend to engage in a kind of spiritual instead of physical flagellation. But whether done subtly or plainly, the idea behind such inflictions is to isolate or destroy the flesh so that the spirit will be able to serve God without hindrance.

But is that a Christian concept? If Christ is to be our true example, it would hardly seem so. The Jews complained about him just because he was not an ascetic! In fact, he was quite unlike their idea of what a holy man should be - see Lu 7:34-35; cp. also 5:37. He mingled freely with people, he ate and drank with pleasure, he dressed finely (cp. Jn 19:23-24).

Even when he instructed his disciples to forsake everything for him, Jesus promised that they would suffer no lack (Mk 10:29-31).

---

[30]  This information about the stylites, and St. Simeon, is taken from the **Dictionary of the Christian church**, ed. J. D. Douglas; Paternoster Press, Exeter, Devon, UK 1974 Articles, "Stylite," and "Simeon the Stylite."

(He added, however, that persecution was inescapable for those who sought to be godly.)

## B) Jesus' Example

It may be objected that Jesus himself claimed poverty saying that he had no home or possessions of his own, and insisting that his disciples follow his example (Mt 8:19-22; Lu 9:57-62). But that state of destitution was true of him only during the three years of his public ministry. It was an inescapable part of that ministry. To fulfil the work his Father had given him, he had to leave his home at Nazareth, his family, his friends. His goal was Calvary, where he was made poor for our sake so that by his poverty we might become rich (2 Co 8:9).

It is true that some of his followers are obliged to make the same kind of total sacrifice of self-interest, even to martyrdom; and it is also true that all of his followers are required to be at least willing to give everything to him. **But in practice, most Christians are released from that supreme demand. They are free to pursue their own lives, and to fulfil their own dreams, providing they do so in a godly way.**

## 2. What About Self-denial?

Some time ago I picked up a document that was being circulated among the people in my church. It had gained a warm response from many of them, and additional copies had been made so that it could have a wider circulation. I have printed this document below, together with my comments. The author of the document is unknown to me.

May I suggest that you cover up my comments and read the document itself first? Assessing your own reaction to it, before looking at mine, may prove to be quite enlightening.

# DYING TO SELF

### The Document

> If we are to know humility, we must be dead to self. When you are forgotten or neglected or purposely set at naught, and you don't sting or hurt with the insult or the oversight, but your heart is happy, that is dying to self.

### My Response

I would say, that is neither humility nor dying to self; rather, it is ceasing to be human altogether. Adoption of that kind of personal negation would turn anyone into a grey blob, colourless, dull, void of the rich, warm emotional content that is a vital part of being truly human. No sensitive and responsive person could fail to be hurt or grieved by purposeful neglect or insult. "Dying to self" does not mean failing to have a natural human response to indignity and malice; but it does mean handling that response in a Christ-like way. That is, you do not return injury for injury, nor insult for insult, but you return love (Ro 12:17-21). That is dying to self.

### The Document

> When your good is evil spoken of, when your wishes are crossed, your advice disregarded, your opinions ridiculed, and you refuse to let anger rise in your heart or even to defend yourself, but take it all in patient, loving silence, that is dying to self.

### My Response

That is to be more pious than Christ himself. Jesus blazed with anger on several occasions; he vigorously defended his personal conduct, his preaching, and his healing ministry; he sternly rebuked those who ignored his counsel; he scornfully denounced those who accused him of being in league with the devil; he publicly embarrassed his opponents and showed that he had small tolerance for religious bigots, or for the proud, the oppressor, and so on.

## The Document

When you never care to refer to yourself in your conversation or to record your own good works, or itch after commendation; when you can truly love to be unknown, that is dying to self.

## My Response

On that criterion you would have to say the apostle Paul never managed to achieve this death to self! How could any person of holy ambition, who yearns to turn his neighbours from the power of Satan to God, and from darkness to light, who hungers to set the captives free, to proclaim the word of God to all and sundry, and to see the church grow mightily, be content "to be unknown"?

Paul boldly recorded what he had done for God, he often referred to himself, he earnestly desired the commendation of the churches, and of all good men, and so does any person who rightly understands the purposes of God. I should think the demons of hell would shout with glee if our unknown author succeeded in persuading all Christians to go off and hide in some self-effacing corner. There is of course no room in the kingdom of God for self-conceit and personal aggrandisement; but there is unlimited room for people of action and drive to go and do exploits for their God (Da 11:32).

## The Document

When you lovingly and patiently bear any disorder and irregularity and unpunctuality, or any annoyance; when you can stand face to face with waste, folly, extravagance, and spiritual insensibility, and endure it, that is dying to self.

## My Response

I would say, that is to allow fools to govern the earth. I have not the slightest intention of passively enduring irregularity, unpunctuality, waste, folly, extravagance, and the like. Where I find such crass behaviour I will do all in my power to rebuke it, prevent it, and, if necessary, punish it. To do otherwise is to mock all good order and discipline and to deny all communal responsibility. To tolerate such things, without anger, and without any attempt to correct them, is not dying to self, rather it is dying to wisdom and duty. Let those who wish to, become accomplices in folly; but let us not say that Christ bids them to do so.

## The Document

When you can see your brother or sister prosper and have his or her needs met, and honestly rejoice with them in spirit, and feel no envy nor question God, while your own needs are far greater, that is dying to self.

## My Response

I agree, but with caution - for if my needs were not being met, while another's were, I probably would question God. I would ask whether the fault were mine? Perhaps I am out of step with God's will? Perhaps my faith needs to be provoked into action? But perhaps also the Lord may want to teach me submission to his providence?

The Document

> When you can receive correction or reproof from one of less stature than yourself, and can submit inwardly as well as outwardly, finding no rebellion or resentment rising up within your heart, that is dying to self.

My Response

I agree; **that** is indeed dying to self.

Apart from the last two paragraphs, the above document seems to me to reflect more a Buddhist concept of the annihilation of personal identity and character, than the Christian concept of "a more abundant life".

There is a deep paganism, a false self-loathing, inherent in the document, as there is also in a large number of devotional writings. Such writings do not reflect Christian values. They look godly on the surface, and they attract many pious readers. But in the end they are a source of spiritual bondage. They imprison the spirits of their devotees. They do not and cannot give the spiritual release they offer. They pretend to honour God, but in reality they dishonour him by departing from the truth of Christ that sets men free.

In contrast with this pagan denial of ordinary human life and its values ...

## 3. <u>God Wants You To Affirm Life</u>

This virtually brings us right back to the beginning of the book - for this has been my aim throughout: **to set before you a Christian life-style that is natural, friendly, positive, cheerful, and Christ-like.**

Let me sum it all up in three statements -

## A) God Wants You To Live Abundantly

Jesus said, "The thief comes only to steal and kill and destroy; I came that they may have life, and have it abundantly" (Jn 10:10). And the apostle who recorded that saying of Christ, showed how he understood it: **"Beloved, I pray that all may go well with you and that you may be in health; I know that it is well with your soul" (3 Jn. 2).**

But many Christians are like the Sydney woman who hired a car with an automatic transmission. She drove it to Melbourne (some 600 miles), and when she arrived complained bitterly to the agent that the vehicle had been slow, the engine noisy, and that it had consumed enormous quantities of fuel. The agent expressed surprise, but agreed to check the car. When he did so, he found the transmission was set in second gear. The lady had not known that she could advance it to top, so she had driven the entire distance in the lower position!

Just so, there are Christians who are grinding along when they should be rising up on eagle's wings (Is 40:29-31); they are grovelling, when they should be standing tall as God's own people, his chosen race, a holy nation, a royal priesthood! (1 Pe 2:9).

## B) God Wants You To Live Naturally

*"He has showed you, O man, what is good; and what does the Lord require of you but to do justice, and to love kindness, and to walk humbly with your God?" (Mi 6:8).*

Micah gives there a capsule description of godly living. It is a picture of the people of God living natural, compassionate, ordinary, humble lives. They are not adopting some spurious or artificial "religious" life-style. They know that would be repulsive to Christ (Mt 6:2,5,16; 18:4-7).

They do not feel a compulsion either to parade their religion before the world or to hide it from the world. They know that their real difference from the world does not lie in the clothes they wear, nor the culture they express, but in their goals and attitudes.

They are content to work and play, laugh and weep, sing and pray, eat and sleep, as the providence of God ordains for each day. They are content to do what comes naturally; yet all the time staying open to the Spirit of God, so that he may change in them whatever may need changing, and plant in them whatever attributes he may wish to.

Such natural Christians walk pleasantly with themselves, kindly with their neighbours, and humbly with their God.

### C) <u>God Wants You To Live Expectantly</u>

*"The Lord is not slow about his promise as some count slowness, but is forbearing toward you, not wishing that any should perish, but that all should reach repentance. But the day of the Lord will come like a thief, and then the heavens will pass away with a loud noise, and the elements will be dissolved with fire, and the earth and the works that are upon it will be burned up. Since all these things are thus to be dissolved, what sort of persons ought you to be in lives of holiness and godliness, waiting for and hastening the coming of the day of God, because of which the heavens will be kindled and dissolved, and the elements will melt with fire! But according to his promise we wait for new heavens and a new earth in which righteousness dwells"* (2 Pe 3:9-13).

CPSIA information can be obtained at www.ICGtesting.com
Printed in the USA
BVOW08s0627270415

397696BV00006B/58/P

9 781615 290369